CW00684311

WE CAN
SWING
TOGETHER

WE CAN SWING TOGETHER

THE STORY OF
Lindisfarne

JOHN VAN DER KISTE

FONTHILL

Fonthill Media Language Policy

Fonthill Media publishes in the international English language market. One language edition is published worldwide. As there are minor differences in spelling and presentation, especially with regard to American English and British English, a policy is necessary to define which form of English to use. The Fonthill Policy is to use the form of English native to the author. John Van der Kiste was born and educated in England; therefore British English has been adopted in this publication.

Fonthill Media Limited
Fonthill Media LLC
www.fonthillmedia.com
office@fonthillmedia.com

First published in the United Kingdom and the United States of America 2017

British Library Cataloguing in Publication Data:
A catalogue record for this book is available from the British Library

Copyright © John Van der Kiste 2017

ISBN 978-1-78155-589-7

The right of John Van der Kiste to be identified as the author of this work has been asserted by him in accordance with the Copyright, Designs and Patents Act 1988.

All rights reserved. No part of this publication may be reproduced, stored in a retrieval system or transmitted in any form or by any means, electronic, mechanical, photocopying, recording or otherwise, without prior permission in writing from Fonthill Media Limited

Typeset in 10.5pt on 13pt Sabon
Printed and bound by CPI Group (UK) Ltd, Croydon, CR0 4YY

Foreword

In the summer of 1972, I was taking my A-levels and preparing to leave school. When not swotting furiously for exams, one of our priorities was to get our hands on the latest weekly issue of *Melody Maker*, *New Musical Express*, or *Sounds*, remaining all the while within a few inches of the stereo and a large collection of albums. With regard to the British music scene at the time, T. Rex had just had what turned out to be the last of their four No. 1 singles, while Slade were just beginning a run of chart-toppers that for a while threatened to rival the Beatles' supremacy in the 1960s; at the same time, Rod Stewart was the top-selling album act, while Elton John and David Bowie were about to launch themselves into the stratosphere, two success stories that would run and run.

Yet the best-selling British album group at the time, by a mile, was Lindisfarne. *Fog on the Tyne* spent twenty weeks in the top ten, four of them at No. 1. Almost everyone I knew at school had a copy. It was to 1972 what *Bridge Over Troubled Water* had been two years earlier, or *Sergeant Pepper's Lonely Hearts Club Band* two or three years before that. Anyone who could play a few chords on acoustic guitar had a shot at the title song as well. Meanwhile, the group also had two top five singles in a row, and were never off the first few pages of the music weeklies, sometimes with the word 'LINDISFARNTASTIC' overhead. To crown it all, in the last few days of our final term that July, a bunch of us stumped up £1.25 each for tickets to see them live at Queen's Hall, Barnstaple, on their summer mini-tour of the UK.

Nothing lasts forever, and Lindisfarne's position as Britain's ultimate group was brief. Over the next few years, they split, reformed with a new line-up, disbanded completely, reunited, lost and added new members, and survived the sudden death of their front man. At the time of writing, Rod Clements's Lindisfarne are still gracing a stage in some concert hall or other, while each of their top ten singles still features regularly on the airwaves.

Here is one lifelong fan's version of the story. I cannot claim it is the first. The group's publicist Dave Ian Hill blazed the trail with *Fog On The Tyne: The Official History of Lindisfarne* in 1998, later revised for Kindle, and I can hardly not tip my hat to his excellent pioneering work. They say that imitation is the sincerest form of flattery, yet I have not sought to imitate his book, merely to present another respectful view of one of British music's most unique collective talents.

I would also like to acknowledge my considerable debt to archive material and interviews on the official Lindisfarne website, particularly two regular contributors, Derek Walmsley and Mike Clayton, for their invaluable advice and, above all, for some excellent photographs and memorabilia used herein; to two old friends, Miles Tredinnick, whose idea it was that I should write this book in the first place, and Ian Herne, whose insights into the group as another long-term fan have provided much useful food for thought; to Rab Noakes, for relevant information; to my wife Kim for her invaluable encouragement, support, and reading through; to Sylvia Hemsil, who also kindly read the manuscript in final draft stage; and to my editors, Jay Slater and Joshua Greenland. Above all, I am extremely grateful to original group members Rod Clements and Ray Laidlaw, for the very helpful and detailed answers they were kind enough to supply to my questions.

In the text and the guest appearances section of the discography, albums, books, films, publications, radio and television programme titles are in italics, while singles and individual tracks are in single inverted commas. All chart positions and statistics are from the Guinness Books of British Hit Singles and Albums, unless otherwise stated.

CONTENTS

Folk Clubs and Brethren

In 1954, popular music and easy listening were very much one and the same. The biggest selling pop singles of the era came from Doris Day, Frankie Laine, Rosemary Clooney, and Frank Sinatra. By 1955, 'Rock Around the Clock' by Bill Haley & His Comets was repeating its American chart-topping status on the other side of the Atlantic as it signalled the shape of things to come, and many a British schoolboy would find inspiration in the new emerging sounds of rock 'n' roll.

Among them were three youngsters in North Shields. Rod Clements, born 17 November 1947 in North Shields, and Simon 'Si' Cowe, born 1 April 1948 in Jesmond, first met when they started at Kings School, Tynemouth, at around the age of five. They were part of the same group of friends or semifriends from the start, although their shared love of music would not rear its head for a while. It began to take shape around 1960 when they met Ray Laidlaw, born 28 May 1948 in North Shields. When Ray was aged twelve, his cousin who lived opposite was friends with another youngster down the street, and was learning guitar. At this time, the major influences on the new generation were Elvis Presley, Lonnie Donegan ('the first King of Britpop', the man to whom guitar playing in Britain could be traced as a popular activity), and Brian Rankin, a teenager from Newcastle just beginning to make good, now finding fame under the name Hank Marvin as guitarist with Cliff Richard and The Shadows.[1] On his ninth or tenth birthday, Si was given a Russian-made Spanish guitar for his birthday, and after that, it was all systems go on learning chords to play along with songs like 'My Old Man's a Dustman'. Ray was given a set of drums for Christmas, and then he joined his first group with Si and his next-door neighbour Giles Bavidge on guitars, plus fellow schoolmate Rob Gray on bass guitar.

Their progress was interrupted when Si started going to boarding school at Fettes College, Edinburgh, where he could lay claim to having formed the first-ever pop group there. Although they did not have a name, they played a concert there at which they did 'Swinging Blue Jeans, that sort of stuff'. He was thrilled when the headmaster came up to him afterwards and told him it was '*very* loud, but very good'. From a representative of the generation to whom rock 'n' roll was part of a culture that sometimes eluded any sort of understanding, this was praise indeed.

As with nearly all boarding schools in the 1960s, rules were strictly enforced, but Si and his group managed to occasionally escape just long enough to play a few gigs in Edinburgh. He borrowed a Burns Black Bison guitar, with a large tremolo arm, which had one disadvantage; if a string snapped, the tension went and all the other strings went out of tune—a severe problem if (or when, as in his case) it happened in the first number. Meanwhile, the group that was having to function back at home without him during term time, now named The Aristokats, was playing regularly around Tynemouth. The high point of their career, such as it was, came at a gig during August in the summer holidays when they were paid 30 shillings each, plus free food and drink. Nevertheless, they did not long survive having a guitarist who was away at boarding school, and they gradually drifted apart.

At around the same time, another of their friends in the area, Bob Sargeant, was playing with a group called The Druids. Ray's father was Bob's mother's butcher, and a close link was formed through the usual parental exchange about their respective children's instruments. Bob and his friend Pete Morton both bought guitars and formed a group, playing several times at Whitley Bay Boys' Club. When Ray joined, the regular bookings became residencies for a while, alongside playing at youth clubs in the North Shields, Tynemouth, and Whitley Bay area once a fortnight. The beat boom had just started, and they were discovering the Chicago blues influences, as well as the homegrown fare of The Beatles, The Rolling Stones, and The Yardbirds among others. Inevitably, the group drifted apart after about a year or so.

One of the major local meeting places was the Calypso Coffee bar in Tynemouth, where Rod Clements was among the regulars. He had been through the usual rite of passage at school with a beat group, The Cyclones, playing contemporary chart fare from the likes of Tommy Roe and Brian Hyland. Now he was beginning to develop an interest in blues through listening to Jimmy Reed and Sonny Boy Williamson records. Part of the time, he was playing with a Newcastle combo, The Bert Brown Showband, whom he had met through an advertisement on the wall of a guitar shop. When not working with them, he had another group of his own, Downtown Faction, a kind of 'messing about with first guitars' affair, for which the line-up was himself on bass guitar, George Robertson on guitar, Chris di Soren on drums, and Richard Squirrel on vocals. Their main gigs were eighteenth birthday parties and similar dates, and they enjoyed a successful season or two before burgeoning adult life took over.

As The Druids had gone the same way, Ray Laidlaw was keen to form another group, which he thought would probably retain the name, and he invited Rod to join. Bob Sargeant and Pete Morton were both interested, and the end result would be almost a reformation of the old line-up. Before long, they became Downtown Faction, as the name was 'available' and they all liked it. Richard Squirrel came back on vocals for a while, but he had just started working for Proctor and Gamble, detergent manufacturers, and left the group when he was posted to Canada. Several other local vocalists and musicians joined, left, and sometimes rejoined. Among them were John Spooner and Billy Mitchell, who would later play a long-lasting role in the saga of various groups in years to come. Another was Jeff Sadler, who was in the same class at school as Mark Knopfler, two friends who had learnt guitar together. Mark used to come to rehearsals, but was too shy and unsure of himself to join in. One local group who were an influence on the Downtown Faction were the Junco Partners, a local blues and soul outfit who formed around this time. Rod and Ray used to go and see them regularly, and according to Ray, they were 'the best band ever to come out of Newcastle and not make it'.

Some of the rehearsals were held at Rod's place, particularly during the summer holidays, once his parents had gone to their second home in Spain. As they left the front door, Ray would recall, the rest of them moved in for the next few weeks via the back one.

All the time, these young musicians were soaking up new influences. By 1965, nearly everyone with any interest in current pop was falling under the spell of Bob Dylan. He had just started becoming popular in Britain with his solo acoustic albums of social comment, before alienating some of his more purist followers—but attracting many new, more open-minded devotees—by going electric and forming a full band. Everything moved on quickly in the world of '60s music. The beat boom had been led by The Beatles, The Searchers, and Gerry and The Pacemakers in Liverpool; The Hollies, Freddie and The Dreamers, and Herman's Hermits in Manchester; The Moody Blues in Birmingham; and the more jazz-blues-influenced Manfred Mann, The Yardbirds, The Kinks, The Who, and, above all, The Rolling Stones in the London area. Newcastle's top group was The Animals, seen by some as the forefathers of British folk-rock with their first two singles, 'Baby Let Me Take You Home' and the transatlantic No. 1 'The House of the Rising Sun'—both arrangements of old traditional songs that had appeared on the first Dylan album. Around the end of 1965, the more adventurous of these began experimenting with more unusual instrumentation and different musical concepts as 'pop' became 'rock', while the others gradually fell out of favour and found a lucrative career on the cabaret or pantomime circuit.

For Downtown Faction, the future was increasingly mapped out by the psychedelia of the Butterfield Blues Band (and to a lesser extent former Animals front man Eric Burdon, who had formed a new group while retaining the name and embraced the ethos of peace, love, and San Francisco), the harmonies of The Mamas and The Papas, The Lovin' Spoonful, and Jimi Hendrix—a young American guitarist whose career only took off in Britain under the management of Chas Chandler, the Animals' former bass guitarist.

Sometimes academic life intruded, and in 1968, Rod needed to take a year out from Downtown Faction to complete his General Arts degree at Durham University. It was part of an agreement with his parents that he would thus be able to go and do what he liked for a profession, but would still have a qualification to fall back on if his first choice of career did not work out. Mr Clements Senior had really wanted his son to be a lawyer. It was a situation that many families of the time would come to know only too well, with parents trying to dissuade their musical offspring from seeking a career in rock 'n' roll and instead pursue a genuine time-honoured profession, summed up in a song co-written and recorded by Albert Hammond a few years later, 'The Free Electric Band': 'They used to sit and speculate upon their son's career—a lawyer, or a doctor, or a civil engineer'.

Meanwhile, Si Cowe, who had led a full and productive school life at Fettes, including building his own guitar in woodwork lessons, was also faced with the dilemma of what to do with himself after A-levels. When he was offered a place at university and it arrived in the post, he hid it unopened beneath the bedroom carpet. Assuming that he had not been accepted, and knowing how keen his son was on photography, his architect father tried to find him a job with a film unit in London, but it fell through as he was not a union member. In order to placate his dad, Si went to work on a building site in North Shields. During his first week there, while he was carrying a bucket of hot bitumen up a ladder, it caught the lip of the roof and spilt on his hands. Both of them fused together, a painful visit to the hospital ensued where they were freed after a couple of hours and he temporarily lost a layer of skin. Luckily, he had used part of his first week's wages to pay his first insurance stamp, and he accordingly received six months' industrial accident benefit. Even more fortunately, he soon recovered completely and was able to pick up the guitar again. Going to London for a while, he took a temporary job as a chef at the RAC Club in Pall Mall, while also catching up with old friends and enjoying a few music sessions.

On his return home, he found another job at Barbecue Express, while answering his father's regular questions as to when he was going to get a proper job with 'I like playing my guitar and doing rock 'n' roll'. His father found him rather better alternative employment at Turner's Photographers, Newcastle, where he spent eighteen months or so learning the craft and joining a film unit. As Mr Cowe Senior had lost his licence, Si had to drive him to his job in the city every day, and one morning he passed Ray Laidlaw at a bus stop. It was the first time they had seen each other for several years, and as they got chatting, Ray mentioned that he was studying art and playing with Downtown Faction, who needed some photos taken and wondered if Si would be interested in the work. It resulted in Si joining the group, initially to deputise on bass guitar when Rod was away, and then playing rhythm guitar when Rod returned as he had fitted in so well. Around the same time, he and Ray set up a blues festival in Leazes Park, Newcastle, the first event of its kind, but offering a more catholic selection of genres than the name might suggest. Sharing the bill with Downtown Faction were The Callies, fronted by Billy Mitchell, and a promising singer-songwriter Alan Hull, born 20 February 1945 at Benwell, Newcastle.

Si's hair was growing long, and his bosses at Turners told him that, as an assistant cameraman, he would have to get it cut and look smart. He did so on stage at Leazes Park, an event which helped them to get some unusual but positive newspaper coverage. Meanwhile, Rod became the social secretary at his college, which enabled him to book national names like Fairport Convention, Wynder K. Frog, and Julie Driscoll with Brian Auger and the Trinity, to say nothing of a regular support slot for Downtown Faction. When people got tired of asking why they always had the same group, Rod would ring the changes and occasionally put the Junco Partners on instead.

As they got better and better, the group started playing gigs outside the north-east, through the Chrysalis agency. They were also invited to do a recording test with Island Records, produced by Guy Stevens who had also worked with Mott the Hoople and Free, and, some ten years later, he would work with The Clash in a similar capacity. Guy was impressed, and told them that he thought they sounded just like Creedence Clearwater Revival, as yet a group of whom very few people in Britain had heard. His overall verdict was that their sound was 'a bit rough at the moment', and they had the potential to make a record but were not quite ready yet. He advised them to keep working at it. As they were packing up, the engineers Mike Bobak and Geoff Gill said they had really liked the music and offered to record them as a way of testing their equipment in 'down time' at Morgan Studios, Willesden. When they went there, owner

Monty Babson liked them so much that he offered them a publishing deal, admittedly not a very lucrative one.

All the same, over the next few months, the group went down to Willesden about eight times, driving seven or eight hours overnight. Sometimes they would arrive to find another group booked in, but when that was not the case, they were able to record long enough to complete tapes for an album. Basically, it was their live set, including early versions of Rod's 'The Road to Kingdom Come' and Si's 'Uncle Sam', both of which would come to fruition on the first two albums. *The Morgan Tapes*, as it was known, remained unreleased, existing solely on acetates in the possession of each member.

When Richard Squirrel left the group, they initially asked Billy Mitchell to join as vocalist, but he turned them down as he intended to continue as a member of The Callies. Then Ray Laidlaw found the ideal replacement. On his way out to lunch one day at the College of Art and Industrial Design, he heard some 'amazing harmonica playing', which seemed to be coming from down the other end of the corridor. The person responsible, sitting in the common room as he accompanied somebody else on guitar, was another musically minded student, Ray Jackson. Born 12 December 1948 in Wallsend, he had been inspired to take up the harmonica when he was ten years old by his grandfather. When he heard Little Walter's harp playing on Bo Diddley's 'Pretty Thing', a single recorded in 1955, and Cyril Davies' 'Country Line Special/Chicago Calling', issued eight years later, Cyril was the first British musician he ever heard playing blues harmonica on record, he knew that was the sound for him.

Ray's other specialty was a more unusual instrument. His parents had first met in Naples during the Second World War, and both being very fond of music from the Neapolitan area, had some records that featured the mandolin. During his late teens, he was fascinated to see Billy J. Kramer and The Dakotas on *Top of the Pops*, playing 'Trains and Boats and Planes'. When it featured a mandolin in the middle section, it was the first time he had ever seen one being played as opposed to just hearing the sound. Shortly afterwards, his parents went on holiday to Italy without him, and to compensate for leaving him behind, they offered to bring him back a present of his choice as a 'peace offering'—he asked for a mandolin. After he had learnt some basic scales, he discovered the music of Woody Guthrie, Cisco Houston, and Sonny Terry playing harmonica and mandolin together.

At school, he formed his first group, The Autumn States. In addition to his skills on mandolin and harmonica, he was also no mean vocalist, having soaked up such diverse influences as The Dillards, Marvin Gaye, Sam Cooke, and John Lennon, particularly the latter. The Beatles, he said, 'were our light', especially on songs like 'Norwegian Wood'. They had written so many songs that 'it was so easy to share in what they were doing. [They tried] to keep the same basic simplicity and honesty in [their] music'.[2] Autumn States, who were more soul-influenced, seemed to be going nowhere, and it took little persuasion on Ray Laidlaw's part to persuade Ray Jackson—who now became 'Jacka' in order to avoid confusion as there were two Rays in the group—to join. Jacka came on board in time to feature on some of the recordings known as *The Morgan Tapes*, including early versions of 'The Road to Kingdom Come', Rod's 'Blues for a Dying Season', 'Uncle Sam', and 'Jimmy's Field', an instrumental they wrote together.

By this time, they had become aware of the growing reputation of one of the soloists who had shared the bill with them at the Leazes Park Festival. Alan Hull had also come from a musical family; his classical music-loving elder sister showed him the rudiments of the piano at home, and when he was eleven, he started to take proper lessons, but soon tired of playing tunes like 'The March of the Tin Soldiers'. Deciding he wanted a guitar, as it was an instrument that one could strum and sing along to, he begged his father for one. Soon after that, courtesy of the BBC Radio Light programme, he discovered 'Rock Around the Clock'. Elvis Presley's 'Hound Dog' was the first record he ever bought, and then he came across Buddy Holly, Chuck Berry, and the rest of the 1950s rock 'n' roll greats. The excitement of rock changed his life, as it did that of so many others of his generation. A reluctant and rebellious schoolboy, he ended his days at Rutherford Grammar rather suddenly by swearing at the headmaster.

Next, he followed the usual rites of passage, joining a couple of groups in his teenage years, firstly The Klik and secondly Dean Ford and The Crestas (the leader of the latter having no connection with the Marmalade vocalist of that name). The group who would launch his recording career, albeit briefly, was The Chosen Few, whom he joined in 1965 on guitar and vocals. With Mickey Gallagher (also formerly from The Klik) on keyboards, Alan 'Bumper' Brown on bass, Rod Hudd on vocals, and Tommy Jackman on drums, they played a few local clubs. Their repertoire consisted of about 60 per cent of Alan's songs, 'about 20% weird Tamla Motown things and about 20% Lovin' Spoonful things', he later recalled: 'We were an enigma at that time because we were playing music and songs rather than freaky guitar solos and that was in 1965'.[3]

Their breakthrough came when manager Bill Keith entered them in a nationwide talent search sponsored by Radio Luxembourg. Alan and Bumper were at the latter's house one evening, working on new songs together, when they received a message to join the others and go along to a local boys' club at an audition organised by Cyril Stapleton, jazz bandleader and now head of Artist & Repertoire for Pye Records. On arrival, they watched and listened to several other groups going through their paces, and at length were told that they would be going on next. As they had brought no gear with them, they needed to use instruments and amps belonging to the previous group. Halfway through the first number, Cyril got up, told them to stop, and asked Alan if he had any more songs up his sleeve. 'Fifty' was the reply, and after they had played another two or three, Cyril invited them to go to London the next day. That was the end of the talent contest.[4]

The Chosen Few promptly signed a contract with Pye Records. Two singles were released that summer, 'I Won't Be Around You Any More' and 'So Much to Look Forward To', with both sides of each written by Alan. In his words, they were 'very Beatlesque'. Although neither of them saw any chart action, there was every likelihood of more, until a difference of opinion with the man who had invited them to London. While they were recording what would probably have been the third single, an angry protest song by Alan, 'This Land Is Called', Cyril objected to some of the lyrics and wanted to change them. Alan refused and Cyril ordered everyone to stop the session—and Alan and Bumper were out of the group. They were replaced by vocalist Graham Bell and guitarist Johnny Turnbull. With a few further line-up changes, The Chosen Few became Skip Bifferty, who made four singles, one under the name of Heavy Jelly, and an album before disbanding. Some members would play significant roles in Alan's career later on.

In August 1966, Alan married Patricia Sharp. As a family man, he needed the income of a steady job, and for about two years, he worked as a psychiatric nurse at St Nicholas Psychiatric Hospital in Gosforth. Far from turning his back on music, he found that the experience enhanced his perception and inspiration as a songwriter—working with 'schizophrenics, depressives and maniacs' gave him ideas for many more songs. Looking back on the whole experience in 1971, in an interview with journalist Roy Carr, he stated: '[The true reflection of a society was] shown in how that society treats its mental cripples because we're all on the brink of going under in a sea of madness'. He could recognise the insanity in himself, and writing songs stopped him going insane: 'It won't be the bomb or some other virus that will destroy the world, but man's own madness'.[5]

Even at this early stage, Alan had a vast collection of original songs to trawl through for his repertoire, as he would recall about twenty years later.

Take your acoustic guitar up to the attic and write, that's exactly what I did. I've always found that even if your mind is blank you can start strumming anything and something will evolve. Maybe not very good at all, but if you keep at it, it gets better and you find yourself in a different world. And if you just let the world come, you'll have a song.[6]

On a lighter note, he once reminisced with another journalist, Bob Edmands, about his days in the nursing profession. 'Neurotics build castles in the sky,' he said, 'psychotics live in them, psychiatrists collect the rent, and psychopaths smash the windows'—cue laughter. He owned up to it being an old gag, but was rather pleased with his own addition of the last bit.[7]

If Tyneside was rich in venues for beat and blues groups, it was also a thriving centre of folk clubs where Alan found his best chances of performing his music with just an acoustic guitar for accompaniment. By late 1968, Cream, who had just disbanded, and Led Zeppelin, who had just formed, were all the rage:

But I just couldn't work out that thing, and most of the bands in Newcastle were playing heavy rock which I didn't understand so the only possible thing to do was get into folk clubs—and so I did with a little bit of success so that I got my own folk club.[8]

He already had Barbara Hayes, who had been working for April Music Publishing and was setting up a new company, Hazy Music, looking after publication of his songs. Now he was starting to do the rounds of the clubs, mostly on his home patch, but occasionally venturing towards London. One venue where he put in a few appearances was Les Cousins, 49 Greek Street, in Soho. Here, audiences generally numbering 150 or less could expect to see up and coming British folk and blues acts, such as Ralph McTell, Donovan, Sandy Denny, Bert Jansch, Cat Stevens, Alexis Korner, Martin Carthy, Dave Swarbrick, and John Martyn, as well as American performers like Paul Simon, Joan Baez, Julie Felix, Arlo Guthrie, and Champion Jack Dupree. It was very much one of the 'in places' to be, and even Pete Townshend, Jimi Hendrix, and Jimmy Page would look in to keep their fingers on the contemporary pulse, as did Joe Boyd, later producer of Fairport Convention, and others checking out the emerging talent. Joe recalled that the formidable Barbara Hayes came in on one occasion to tell them that they really ought to give this new Northern singer-songwriter Alan Hull a chance. It was largely thanks to her that he was able to perform there on occasion, and went down well—although he was clearly very nervous, doubtless ill at ease at being so far from familiar territory.

It was also her knocking on metaphorical doors that led to him releasing a first solo single in the summer and autumn of 1969, 'We Can Swing

Together'. He had been inspired to write the song after an abortive raid on a party in Newcastle in September 1967, attended by several art students including Ray Jackson and John Porter, a future Roxy Music producer. At about 4 a.m., there was a loud thumping on the doors and members of the constabulary with dogs forced their way in, shoved everyone up against the walls, and a few people were physically threatened. Everyone was drunk and there was still plenty of alcohol on the premises. The host sued the police force and was awarded damages. Alan was not present, but after being told about it, he wrote the song, which related a slightly different outcome to the story in which the partygoers were handcuffed, put on trial, and sent to prison by the County Judge, only for the defendants to hear him sing the chorus 'we can swing together, cause we know we're doing it right' under his breath in solidarity with them as they were escorted to their cells.

Nat Joseph, the founder of Transatlantic Records, was suitably impressed. Recorded in a swift session at Trident Studios in St Anne's Court, off Wardour Street, with Albert Lee on guitar, Clem Cattini on drums, and 'sixth Rolling Stone' Ian Stewart on piano, and produced by Hugh Murphy, the result was a cheerily rough and ready debut recorded in an afternoon and mixed the next morning, as was the B-side, 'Obidiah's Grave'. Alan was not impressed with the result, considering it 'a pretty bad recording because it was done with session men and wasn't very inspired'.[9] Although Alan Freeman proved supportive of the record on Radio 1's *Pick of the Pops*, it may have been a little left-field for more general daytime airplay, and its unashamed establishment-baiting character doubtless proved too much for the majority of radio producers. Songs about true stories of taking on the police and actually winning were few and far between. However, one concession to legal niceties had to be made, mainly at Hugh's suggestion, with a change of lyric in the first verse from 'rolling up joints' to 'roll your owns', to keep the Director of Public Prosecutions and the spectre of an outright BBC ban at bay. Yet it enabled Alan to put down a marker for the start of what would be a remarkable career, in artistic if not commercially successful terms, stretching over the next quarter of a century.

At around this time, Alan's path began to cross with that of the individual members of Brethren. He met Ray at one or two studio sessions and they briefly put a group together. The Gift were an outfit who came together spontaneously, with Johnny Turnbull and Graham Bell from the ashes of the shortlived Skip Bifferty. Ray was still first and foremost a member of Downtown Faction, and recognised at once that The Gift were 'a complete shambles'. In his view, Alan was the only one with any really lasting talent, and he felt that some kind of collaboration with him, involving Downtown Faction as well, would be the obvious outcome.

Another influential figure in the background was studio owner Dave Wood, who had invited Alan to come and do some demos at his studio and ended up becoming his manager for a while. Between them, they decided to set up a folk club in the café of the Rex Hotel on the seafront at Whitley Bay. It became a regular fixture on Sunday nights, when they set up a PA system, charged 10s on the door, and staged amateur nights where anybody could come along and perform. There were floor singers and main guests, including Ralph McTell, Al Stewart, and The Humblebums—a duo consisting of Billy Connolly and Gerry Rafferty, who charged £30 per appearance. It became something of a northern equivalent of Les Cousins, although it never attracted such a diverse clientele of stars in the making as its more famous London counterpart. Even so, it went a long way towards explaining the more northern, less Anglo-American nature of Alan's writing, and he always looked back on the simplicity of those days with affection. When he had hit the big time, he still sometimes hankered for the more informal scene he had left behind:

> Folk clubs are pure camaraderie, the best underground in the world. When you talk in terms of commerciality it's nowhere. It's just a nice thing to do instead of being on a bus, going all round the world and playing to thousands of people.[10]

Throughout his career, comparisons were made between Alan and Bob Dylan, and his idol John Lennon. Some two decades on, one writer took issue with those who considered that his writing was to Tyneside what Lennon and McCartney's had been to Liverpool. He maintained that Alan's writings had more in common with those of Ray Davies, and their 'sense of place' being stronger than that of The Beatles. The comparison was an apt one, for a number of The Kinks' main man's songs were firmly rooted in or around the Muswell Hill area of London, in which he had been born and raised, while the majority of Alan's always bore an authentic Newcastle stamp through and through.[11] With the exception of 'Penny Lane' and 'Strawberry Fields Forever', few, if any, of The Beatles' songs really reflected life in their home city. Jacka said that all of Lindisfarne were proud of their northern roots: 'In the most popular period of the band's history we always had our feet close to the ground and were not impressed much by the business'.[12]

The Rex club rapidly became so popular that any such fees were more than covered. Ralph was more than ready to encourage this burgeoning talent, and Alan plus the musicians who would later become Lindisfarne were so appreciative of his support that they called him 'Uncle Ralph'—a name that stuck. According to Ray Laidlaw, the club had a relatively relaxed musical policy, in contrast to the establishments, which prided themselves on being bastions of British traditional folk and were liable to give anything that deviated from that the cold shoulder; at the Rex Club, performers could do anything within reason, as long as they did not bring a full PA along with them.

Alan had left his job as a mental nurse and was now on the dole. With a wife and three small daughters to support, money was essential. As his manager, Dave was paying him £10 a week, and when he was not playing, he made a living cleaning windows for cash. Yet the music was beginning to reap some financial dividends. At around the time that Downtown Faction changed their name to Brethren, they were booked to play the Rex Club for £3. Ray Laidlaw had dispensed with the drum kit for a while and played tambourine, while the others had also gone 'unplugged' with their acoustic guitars, fiddle, banjo, and double bass. The door money was so good that Alan ended up making £30 on the night. He held a raffle and Rod Clements won the prize—a Bert Jansch album. It had been Alan's own copy, but he did not mind when he saw the evening's takings afterwards.

As for Brethren themselves, Alan was spellbound. A group who had previously been going with the flow and first of all playing beat music, then taken the journey into 12-bar blues and psychedelic music, had now gone acoustic. After one of their performances, he reportedly approached them to say he had 'a few songs' that might fit in with what they were doing, if they would like to give him a try sometime. His version of their original meeting was slightly different: 'They came along and said "Can we play at your folk club?" and I said "Yeah, as long as you buy me a pint." And so they played and they were great'.[13]

Contact thus established, they linked up for a jam the following week. Brethren had found that heavy rock was becoming the order of the day, with Led Zeppelin, Free, Ten Years After, the recently disbanded Cream (and their shortlived successor group Blind Faith), and Status Quo (formerly a psychedelic pop outfit now turning towards blues and boogie) all very much in fashion. Brethren were finding gigs harder to come by, although audiences loved the folk blues element in their set, Jacka having brought along the Sonny Terry & Brownie McGhee and the Woody Guthrie influences in. Although they were not to know, down south in the London area another group of young hopefuls, The Good Earth, had also just morphed from an amplified beat group to a drummerless combo. They played a distinctive brand of good-time blues, whose repertoire and original material owed much to Woody Guthrie and Leadbelly, and were about to leave their mark on the first year of the next decade as Mungo Jerry. Both groups were thumbing their nose at the prevailing trends, and finding that live audiences were generally appreciative of their spontaneous style as well, as Rod later recalled:

> We definitely saw ourselves as the antithesis of over-serious Zep/Sabbath style hard rock, prog pretentiousness and glam posturing, and Mungo Jerry were obviously kindred spirits with their evident jug-band and folk-blues roots. I'd count McGuinness Flint as soulmates in that respect too.[14]

Ray agreed wholeheartedly with this verdict:

> We took our music seriously but didn't take ourselves seriously. We enjoyed performing and it showed. That set us apart from most of the other groups. We did feel very protective of the band's songwriting reputation and felt we were a cut above most of our contemporaries.[15]

Scottish singer-songwriter Rab Noakes, who had been part of the 'Fife mafia' that also comprised Billy Connolly, Gerry Rafferty, and The JSD Band, became a close friend, and the group used some of his songs in their repertoire.

As they began using more of Alan's numbers as well, the next logical move came for him to join on a permanent basis. At least one of his future colleagues had some reservations. While acknowledging that Alan was undoubtedly a very talented writer and poet—'and didn't he let you know it'—according to Jacka, 'he was arrogant, belligerent and insolent to everyone who came within his circle of influence'.[16] With hindsight, he admitted that it was probably a defence mechanism, but on first acquaintance, it seemed that Alan was not always the easiest of people to get on with. Billy Mitchell was rather more charitable:

> [Alan] was the first singer that came along and played all his own songs. No covers—just his distinctive material. In those days he was loud, boisterous and vocal, but he had a great energy and enthusiasm which won you over. Alan could be awkward, but that always sprang from a deep belief in what he was doing or trying to say.[17]

Bill Keith, owner of an influential beat club on the quayside of Newcastle and Dave Wood, who had the only serious recording studio on Tyneside in the '60s, both believed strongly in Alan's talent, offering him rehearsal facilities, gigs, and free recording time. Unfortunately, opined Jacka, it only added to his inflated ego and did not go down at all well with the other struggling musicians around at the time. However, once they got to know him and realised he would never buy anyone a pint, 'he was not all bad'.[18] Once it was decided that he should join forces with Brethren and they had got over their apprehension about having this uncompromising character in the fold, they accepted his insistence at being promoted as Alan Hull and Brethren wherever they played, mainly as he had already released a solo single. As lead vocalists, he and Jacka jointly shared the role of front man and learned to complement each other. After a while, they dropped Alan's billing and just became Brethren.

Three of Dave's recordings from the early days made it on to vinyl. 'Positive Earth' (written by Si) and another version of 'We Can Swing Together' were taped by Brethren, as was a solo song by Alan, 'Where Is My Sixpence?' They appeared on *Take Off Your Head and Listen*, which was a sampler album on the Rubber label launched in Newcastle in 1971 alongside tracks by The Callies and Hedgehog Pie. However, by the time the record was released and in the shops, time had marched on and Brethren were but a distant memory.

'Fog on the Tyne'

Towards the end of 1969, Brethren played their first gig with Alan as a full member at the Lampglass in Ashington. A potent musical force had just arrived, and would within three years be one of the most successful acts on the British music scene.

Brethren and their manager Joe Robertson had already been actively seeking a record deal, as had Alan with help from Barbara Hayes and Dave Wood. Though the story of how the initial approach was made depends on which source one believes, it was apparent that Barbara contacted Tony Stratton-Smith, a former journalist who had just founded his own company, Charisma Records. In 1969 and 1970, the British music industry was notable partly for a diverse range of new labels, all catering for what was tagged as the progressive market. Some were launched by the major companies, notably EMI's Harvest, Philips/Fontana's Vertigo, and Pye's Dawn. Others were small independents sometimes started by managers, often because they could not obtain a deal for a new release by one of their artists. Charisma came about largely because Stratton-Smith, generally known as Strat, was keen to issue an album by the still unsigned Van der Graaf Generator. Like Brian Epstein, Kit Lambert, and Robert Stigwood, Strat was one of a select few entrepreneurs who, said Ray, were making up the rules as they went along and 'lightened up the British music industry in the late '60s and early '70s with their charm, wit and intelligence'.[1] As a former sports journalist, opera lover, biographer, and novelist, he was something of a Renaissance man in the showbiz world. He personally throve on the insecurity and adventure of such an undertaking, saying that running an independent record label was 'a gambler's business' and 'not for bankers or investment people'.[2]

There is also more than one version of events as to how the group secured their first recording contract. Jacka and others later recalled that Strat's interest had been aroused after listening to their demo tape, he was particularly impressed with his harmonica work and declared he could make Jacka the next Ian Anderson. Every self-respecting music impresario and punter looked up to rock music's foremost singer-flautist, the front man of Jethro Tull. Even so, he was not sufficiently convinced to sign them on the strength of the tape alone, and also wanted to see them deliver the goods live. He asked them to play a gig at the Marquee in Wardour Street, Soho. Alan Hull & Brethren drove down the A1 from Newcastle in a short wheel base Transit van early on the morning of Sunday 31 May 1970 to play that afternoon as support to American country rock outfit Daddy Longlegs. The journey was a potentially hazardous business, as were several more like it during the next few months. When they were travelling, the prime position was for each one to take it in turns to get on top of the PA columns at the back of the van and lie in the space under the roof; Jacka reminisced:

> This was never more than a nine-inch gap, but it was the only way you could stretch out. We would negotiate two-hour periods of this cosseted space amongst us, until we reached the venue. I now shudder to think of how dangerous a practice that was and how lucky we were never to be involved in a serious accident.[3]

It was the first of what would be their many appearances at the venue. For any up-and-coming group, the Marquee was the place to play. Several of their heroes, like The Rolling Stones, The Who, and Howlin' Wolf, had already done so. The Marquee and the Speakeasy were the two hubs of the music industry at the time, and anybody who wanted their career prospects to improve had to play and to be seen at them. They were never quite sure what would happen on stage, as there was often an air of informality when jam sessions occurred through visiting musicians being invited to get up and play or sing. On one of their gigs there, they were joined onstage by Paul Rodgers from Free, who got up to sing with them. However, the Marquee was not exactly what they had expected, and when they walked in for the first time, they were astonished to find how scruffy and downmarket it looked. They once said they had 'better-looking gigs in Newcastle', but what it lacked in décor, it more than made up for in atmosphere.

Soon other groups were supporting them, including Every Which Way, Greasy Bear, and Stealers Wheel. Only the last-named, which at the time included Scottish singer-songwriters Gerry Rafferty, Joe Egan, and briefly Rab Noakes, would go on to greater things. As the headlining attraction, they were spared the purgatory of being the support act, and the problems that went with it. Once they came down from Newcastle to open for Ginger Baker's Air Force, only to be told on arrival that the former Cream drummer had refused to let any of his equipment be moved aside, not even for the support act. Two members of his group, Kenny Craddock and Colin Gibson, both of whom would become part of the Lindisfarne family, were so embarrassed that they took them to the bar and did their best to compensate for the major disappointment. During their conversation, Ray later recalled, they were asked by the Marquee management if they would moderate their rather loud comments concerning their opinion of Ginger and his parents' marital status, 'which [they] interjected at every opportune moment'.

Jacka recalled that their performances at The Marquee were mixed from the front row by the roadie, the stage being so small that there was only room for the performers and their gear. In those days, they had no monitor wedges for vocals and everything they heard came back at them from the wall behind the audience. However, it was no problem as it was what they were used to at the time—everybody's ears adjusted to the acoustics very quickly, and, as was often the case in these situations, the more they drank, the better it sounded:

> The dressing room behind the stage could only be described as a corridor. There was no wash basin or toilet behind the stage, so apart from tuning up, there was no earthly reason to be there. When the band first played The Marquee, the bar was at the back of the room in a space opposite the toilets, it was only later on our return visits that they built a bar to the right of the stage in a separate room. The bar was double glazed with unbreakable wire mesh glass to keep the noise from the stage to a minimum, but you could still see the stage. Conversation could take place as the sound from the stage was kept to a minimum. Consequently, many a review of a band's performance by a music journalist was written from there, without them ever going out to catch the atmosphere in the auditorium.[4]

Strat was impressed with their performance, but he was still not yet convinced about their potential, until after a meeting with one of Brethren's joint managers, Joe Robertson—the other being Dave Wood. Joe had taken some of their demos with him when he met Strat to discuss compensation for the loss of Charlie Harcourt, the guitarist with the Junco Partners, the other band he was managing. One of several musicians who had played informally with Alan on previous occasions, Charlie had just left the Juncos to join Jackson Heights, a new group formed by Newcastle-born Lee Jackson, formerly bass guitarist with the recently disbanded The Nice. Jackson Heights were managed by Strat and signed to Charisma, as had been The Nice in their final days. Strat listened to the Brethren demos, accordingly invited them to play a slot on one of his Charisma nights at the Marquee, and offered them a deal after seeing them there.

A slight variation in detail on this story was later revealed to Ray by Greg Burman, an old friend, leader of the Greg Burman Soul Band and also a manufacturer of guitar amps in Newcastle in the 1960s. He told him that when Jackson Heights were getting together, Lee Jackson asked him to supply the band with a set of new amps. Greg went to London to meet Strat so they could discuss the new equipment and payment details. During the meeting, Strat asked him what was going on in Newcastle and were there any bands worth checking up on. Greg spoke about Brethren in glowing terms, and Strat arranged to fly up to Newcastle to see them at the next available gig. A few days later, Greg picked up Strat from the airport and drove him to the Mayfair Ballroom, where they watched the group deliver a storming set, and then drove him straight to the airport back for his flight home. When Joe arrived with the demo tape a few weeks later, Strat already knew all about them. He agreed to have a listen, gave them a gig knowing exactly what their potential was, and proceeded to negotiate 'a not particularly favourable deal' with Joe and Dave that gave the impression he was doing them a favour. Another version had it that Joe would not release Charlie from his managerial contract with the Juncos to join Jackson Heights, unless Strat agreed to sign Brethren as well.

Shortly before first meeting Strat, Brethren had done a recording test at Abbey Road studios for the Air Group of companies, owned by George Martin. The producer in charge, Chris Thomas, had started as an assistant to George while the latter was working with The Beatles. They hit it off at once, and Alan was particularly thrilled to be playing the same harmonium that John Lennon had used on 'We Can Work it Out'. By the time Chris offered them a deal, the approach from Charisma was close to being signed and sealed. The group, or most of them, had taken immediately to Strat, and decided that Charisma felt like a small family, very homely and non-corporate. They had also been offered a management deal by Chas Chandler, who had severed his business ties with an increasingly self-indulgent Jimi Hendrix and was now about to oversee the meteoric rise of Slade, but again they preferred the alternative option. With hindsight, they felt, from a career point of view, they might have done better to have had separate management, but at the time, a one-stop-shop seemed simpler. Yet whatever Strat's faults, he was one of the rock 'n' roll pioneers who was still exploring uncharted territory. 'I'm sure he made some tactical mistakes that cost us a few quid,' Ray said later, 'but there's no guarantee that we would have fared any better with other management/labels.'[5]

The one exception to the general chorus of approval surrounding Strat came from Si. He was annoyed when their driver Pete Haskell went into the office at Charisma one day to ask for more money for 'his lads', and a cost-conscious Strat immediately dispensed with his services.

Back on their home territory, on 2 July, they made their debut at a venue—Newcastle City Hall—that would feature more strongly than any other in their career over the next few years as support to Jackson Heights. Publishing deals were concluded, and then rehearsals for the first album began. With John Anthony producing, sessions took place at Trident Studios, Soho, from 10 to 14 August. While they were there, they bumped into George Harrison, who was recording his triple album *All Things Must Pass* at the same time. The former Beatle was nursing a bleeding finger and muttering crossly in a thick Scouse accent about 'bloody roadies' who were cutting his guitar strings too short.[6]

Five days of recording (from 10 to 14 August) saw twelve songs on tape and ready for remixing three weeks later. At around the same time, they found out that a New York group were also called Brethren, and a change of name was in order. During the sessions, John suggested they call themselves Lindisfarne. Despite some reservations, they agreed that the north-eastern connotations of the holy island worked well, and Lindisfarne they accordingly became. Ironically, the American Brethren lasted less than a couple of years, and their keyboard player Mike Garson was remembered less for his contributions to the group than for his regular work on David Bowie sessions over subsequent years.

The album was named *Nicely Out of Tune* as they considered that it summed up their status with the rest of the music scene—their being 'nicely out of tune with what everyone else was doing'. Inevitably, the majority of the songs (seven) were written by Alan, with two contributions from Rod, plus one from Rab Noakes ('Turn A Deaf Ear'), and Woody Guthrie's 'Jackhammer Blues'. Of Alan's numbers, 'Lady Eleanor', which began side one, was considered the outstanding track. It was a haunting tune, inspired partly by the stories of Edgar Allan Poe, given instrumental colour by the effective contrast of Rod's bass and Alan's shimmering organ, joined later by Jacka's atmospheric mandolin before Alan's vocal came in. Another track, 'Clear White Light—Part 2', was named thus as Alan had written another song with the same title. A number with spiritual overtones, it featured more of the classic three-part vocal harmonies, particularly on the acappella opening. 'Winter Song' was an angry social comment piece, with a bleak lyric about the downtrodden and the homeless, all the more effective for being set to a simple backing of acoustic guitar, Rod's bass and nothing else. Like 'We Can Swing Together'—which appeared in a new and slightly longer version (over five and a half minutes) with Jacka singing the first verse and ending in al fresco choir on the final choruses of friends, flatmates, and anybody else who happened to be passing, plus somebody doodling on a synthesizer—it was an accurate indication of the radical subject matter articulated so fiercely in much of his future work. Lest anybody should think that Alan's songs lacked humour, it was amply disproved by 'Down', a curious barbershop-like ditty that started with a crackly sound designed to sound like an old 78-rpm disc, and Jacka blowing raspberries—hence a credit on the sleeve for 'flatulette'. Another almost-novelty came in the shape of 'Alan in the River With Flowers', the title being an affectionate spoof of The Beatles' 'Lucy in the Sky With Diamonds', sung by Jacka with strange sound effects from vocals being put through a Leslie speaker. When the record was released in America on the Elektra label, someone took exception to the Beatleish title and renamed it 'Float Me Down the River'.

One of Rod's two songs on the record, 'The Road to Kingdom Come', written during his third year at Durham University, was as close to rock as the album came. Like the lighthearted 'Jackhammer Blues', it came with a gritty guitar sound driven by a combination of violin, mandolin, and harmonica. As well as becoming a regular stage favourite, it laid down a pattern whereby Jacka would generally take the lead vocal on songs written by Rod.

The record sleeve featured a monochrome photo of the group outside the Houses of Parliament taken one lunchtime between gigs, inside a frame lifted from a Victorian music book, the whole topped by the group logo in Gothic script. Credits on the back of the sleeve paid ample testimony to the members' multi-instrumental abilities, with Rod not only playing bass guitar and violin, but also organ, piano, and guitar, while Alan was featured on acoustic and twelve-string guitars, organ, piano, and electric piano, and Si on lead, acoustic and twelve-string guitars, mandolin, and banjo. To this day, some admirers maintain that throughout their lengthy career, in terms of recording quality and spirit, Lindisfarne never quite surpassed this debut album.

By now, the group had moved to London, and although Alan and Rod had wives and children there, they still had gigs to honour in the north-east, so they were travelling to and from the capital. One time, they were delayed when their transport, a pre-war low mileage Co-operative Funerals car, let them down badly; they arrived at the studio at 8 p.m.—five hours late. As they did not have anybody's phone numbers, they had been unable to warn of their late arrival, and all they achieved that evening was one backing track. Next morning, they were given a severe dressing down by Strat for wasting everybody's time, apart from the anxiety occasioned him and John who had both wondered whether they had had some dreadful accident. The vehicle that had been responsible promptly went back to the garage whence it came and a more reliable replacement was duly supplied. That unforeseen problem apart, recording of the album went pretty smoothly. They had been playing most of the songs live regularly, everyone pitched in with ideas, and there was little more to be done than to capture everything on tape and then to vinyl with the minimum of embellishment—and, as John would recall, the consumption of several crates of Brown Ale.

The decision to leave Newcastle for the south-east had meant much soul-searching. The whole band wanted, or rather needed, to move to London. Two years later, once they had achieved success, Alan looked back on the predicament they had faced in those early days:

> At that time, it was very frustrating in Newcastle for them because they were so talented and they got an awful recording deal, and they used to come to Dave [Wood]'s studio and I used to be there making frustrated little demos and not really bothering and they used to come in and phone London and ask when their album was coming out, and they always got bullshit replies. So we came together through frustration and through love, and after we came together it was obvious we'd better get down to London. But they'd always thought that, so eventually we arrived in London though it was hard at first being separated from our families. I think everybody in Lindisfarne at that time had an inner feeling, a very quiet confidence that it would be all right one day, sooner or later. And the hassles didn't bother us, we used to go and sleep on friends' floors and lots of good people used to put us up, and we just kept on doing it with this same quiet confidence; I can't really express the feeling, but we just knew it and the money then didn't matter much and it doesn't matter much now.[7]

Living in the capital with the dream of making it meant they had to live on their wits for much of the time, to say nothing of the accidental bounty of others. The streets were not paved with gold, but there were opportunities to be had for those who kept their eyes open. Charisma would put them up in a cheap hotel and pay their food and expenses, but there was no additional spending money, so they would get Strat to sign them in at the Speakeasy, the renowned West End showbiz watering hole, and buy them a drink. The place was usually full of drunken stars who would pull their hankies out and send a shower of cash, often including a few fivers, on the floor. Whenever it happened, five penurious but eager Geordies instantly scooped them up. Their unwitting benefactors also tended to fall asleep over their meals, so they would help themselves to what was left on the plates. They lived like that for about a year, Ray admitted: 'We never felt part of it—we always felt like outsiders'.[8] Even at the peak of their success about eighteen months later, and once they had found their own places in North London close to the A1 for a few years, they were still only on £50 per week, a fair sum of money in those days, but certainly not riches beyond anybody's wildest dreams.

Above all, it was a bit of a culture shock, but they were adamant that living in London would never change them. Alan noted on behalf of them all:

> It's like a separate country, the North East. I miss it. I've not moved my family down yet. If they live down here perhaps I won't miss it so much. I think bands that come from raw areas should be raw—the namby-pamby groups that come from Newcastle just fail.[9]

On release in October, the album received very good reviews in the press, although initial sales were not enough to trouble the lower reaches of the album charts for over a year. Hand in hand with appreciation of the album went a respect for Lindisfarne as a result of their live appearances. They were not only becoming known in the north-east and at the Marquee, but also at Barnstaple, Devon (where they opened for Yes at the Queen's Hall), at a Manchester University show (where they met Fairport Convention (and may or may not have been supporting them—the participants' memories were hazy when they came to recall the occasion) and both groups ended up socialising at an after-hours party), and at the National Jazz and Blues Festival at Plumpton Race Track, Sussex, the forerunner of what would become the annual Reading Festival a year later.

Strat's assistant, Glen Colson, said there was a palpable air of excitement whenever Lindisfarne were playing. They were like a breath of fresh air with their honest approach, mainly acoustic guitars, great songs and melodies, one or two traditional Geordie songs to sing and clap along to, and a general feelgood atmosphere—the polar opposite of groups like King Crimson and Genesis (though he might have done better to choose an example who were not also signed to Charisma). An instrumental break did not mean a five-minute guitar solo, but a burst of mandolin, fiddle, harmonica, banjo, or occasionally a guitar riff—or a riotous combination of the lot. To him, they were 'like a scruffy, folky Beatles'. Other journalists at around the same time picked up on the 'folk-rock Beatles' tag. It had only been months since rock music's favourite Liverpool sons had made their irrevocable parting of the ways public, and music journalists were falling over themselves in their pursuit of 'the new Beatles'. For many of them, it was another group from the north, albeit the north-east, with a quiverful of catchy, easily memorable songs that were superior to the chart-orientated teenage fodder emanating from semi-manufactured groups who did not necessarily play on the singles credited to them, embellished by distinctive vocal harmonies, and above all two front men and not one. Some groups in those circumstances might have found the 'folk-rock Beatles' tag tiresome, but for them it was flattering.

British folk-rock groups were a comparatively new phenomenon. During the mid-'60s, the more commercial side of folk music had been the preserve of acts like The Spinners and The Seekers, both of whom embodied enough musical purity and commerciality to make them favourites for prime-time family entertainment and the easy listening audience on television. The more radical counterpart of folk was represented by names such as Bert Jansch (seen as a British Bob Dylan), John Renbourn, and Ewan MacColl. Towards the end of the decade, the only other major names were Fairport Convention, with their mix of British traditional music, their raids on the Dylan songbook, and songs from their guitarist Richard Thompson, and the as-yet lesser-known Pentangle (formed by Jansch and Renbourn) and The Strawbs.

In show business, the pioneers in their field nearly always have a struggle for acceptance. As David Bowie later remarked, 'it doesn't matter who does something first—it's who does it second that people pay attention to'.[10] In Lindisfarne's case, it was partly because many punters did not really know what to make of them. Alan summed it up pithily:

> [We were] a ludicrously different band and people used to look at us and think 'no guitarist, where's Eric Clapton?' They'd wonder what a mandolin was, and they used to walk away.[11]

Occasionally, the lead instrument was a guitar, although sometimes it was a mandolin or a fiddle. For music fans brought up on beat groups with guitars, drums, maybe keyboards and brass, but nothing else, it was the shock of the new or at least the unconventional.

To take Beatles comparisons further, it gradually became apparent that the convivial Alan was like a Tyneside John Lennon, shaking his fist at the establishment, the acerbic social commentator who cared passionately for the underdog, the one who could put his closest colleagues or former associates down with an ill-considered remark—and, after a period of reflection, be full of apologies towards the wounded party. Jacka came across as the friendly, outgoing, and instantly likeable one, the Paul McCartney of the group. Rod and Si vied for the George Harrison role, both gifted yet underused, somewhat overshadowed songwriters and musicians who would only later have the chance to exploit their potential more fully. Or maybe Si was the Ringo Starr character, the one who had never let fame go to his head and could be guaranteed to shrug anything off with a quip or some similar gesture to prove he never took it seriously.

Throughout his career with the group, he was renowned for rarely signing an autograph with his own name. Once, he confessed, he cheated and signed himself 'Isaac Hite' all night when somebody suggested it as he liked it so much.[12]

Rod was well aware of the George Harrison comparison and admitted he was 'honoured' by it. With George, Dave Davies of The Kinks, and many others, he shared 'the mixed blessing of having been in a band with highly driven and seriously talented songwriters and possibly not being driven or competitive (or talented) enough to give them a run for their money'.[13]

In the early days, Si—who would some two decades later leave the music business to work in a brewery—used to arrange beer trips for them all. Sometimes this involved contra-deals on the road, by which small companies swapped complimentary tickets to gigs in exchange for real ale to be provided in the dressing room. His favourite drinking den was the Magnesia (or 'Maggie') Bank pub above the Fish Quay in North Shields, to the extent that it soon became known as their more-or-less official headquarters because they spent so much of their time there. He later recalled that once they set off on a tour from the Maggie Bank, heading down south for their first show, and someone had had the foresight to arrange a visit to Theakstons' Brewery: 'It was the only time in the whole history of the band that the bus left on time—in fact everybody was there half an hour early!'[14]

Sometimes life could indeed be a party, as on the occasion when Charisma celebrated the company's first birthday at a special bash at the Marquee. After he had been down the West End of London shopping in the afternoon, Si arrived early before the festivities were due to start, sat in the bar having a pint, and watched caterers putting the finishing touches to a birthday cake—decorated with the Mad Hatter company logo in icing—on the main table. After they had gone, leaving a large white cloth draped over the cake in readiness for the grand unveiling, he felt a tap on his shoulder as a voice said, 'Allo, my name's Keef. Fancy giving me a hand to lose that cake?' It was Keith Moon, who had also shown up early. Between them, they hid it under a table and replaced it with a cardboard replica. At the party, just before it was time for the speeches and cake, Strat decided to check under the cloth at the cake (one can never trust these rock musicians) and was not amused. The two culprits immediately confessed and put the genuine article back. Later on, Glen Colson told Si that what he should have done was to replace the cake with Keith: 'When Strat ceremoniously pulled off the cloth, you should have come running down the table and leapt over him. Then the *Melody Maker* could have run the story: "The Cowe jumped over the Moon!"'[15]

By the end of 1970, they were, in the eyes of many, the folk-rock Beatles indeed. Folk music, once immortally dubbed by Billy Connolly as 'bearded men wearing Aran jumpers singing about dead sailors', was basically a broad church, but once thus tagged, it was a mighty hard label to shift.[16] Even long after Bob Dylan had abandoned his one-take recordings featuring only his voice, acoustic guitar, and harmonica for the more diverse styles to be heard on *Blonde On Blonde* and *Nashville Skyline*, music and drama libraries would still file Dylan LPs in the folk music rack. Some forty years later, music journalist and historian Rob Young would note in an account of British folk music that 'Lindisfarne created pub rock as played in an Elizabethan inn'.[17]

'Clear White Light—Part 2' was released as a single in November. Even in a Top 30 where such disparate, un-poppy 45s as Matthews Southern Comfort's 'Woodstock' and the Jimi Hendrix Experience's 'Voodoo Chile' could reach the summit, it was perhaps not potential chart fare, although again the reviews were favourable. *Sounds*, the newest of the music weeklies and an immediate fervent champion of the group, called the vocals 'very Lennonesque' and predicted that they were going to have 'a monstrous hit on their hands', although it would take another couple of ventures on vinyl to fulfil this. The same paper warmly embraced *Nicely Out of Tune*, its reviewer Jerry Gilbert noting that it was rare to hear an album by a new group and decide on one hearing that every track was a potential hit single—'a straight, simple group effort with catchy, easily-memorable songs which were so typical of the early days of the Mersey boom'.[18] Jerry had been one of the first journalists to sing the group's praises and predict how successful they would be as he saw them progress from support band at the Marquee to national headliners.

When he first saw the band at the Marquee, in September 1970, Jerry and Strat took their place in what the former called 'the painfully sparse arena', and perhaps because he had always attached great importance to the tenet of song construction (melodically and rhythmically), he immediately took to the group. What appealed to him above all was a 'nice fat acoustic sound which was so erratic and carefree it immediately took [him] back to [his] old worn Sonny Terry/Woody Guthrie records', especially when they played Woody's 'Jackhammer Blues'. A few weeks later, while they still seemed to be struggling to make any impact, he noticed they were back at the Marquee: 'I recall unhesitatingly singing along with half the songs as though I'd heard them twenty times.' He was not their only early music press cheerleader. Over at sister publication *Melody Maker*, Michael Watts hailed *Nicely Out of Tune* as 'an album which for clarity of style bids fair to establish them as a top band for 1970'.[19]

At the same time, Lindisfarne were finding themselves one of those acts that appealed to the producers of Radio 1 evening shows, just as the demarcation lines between pop and 'progressive' were slowly crumbling. When they recorded an audition tape for *Night Ride*—the late night Radio 1 show—it was passed by the panel with a comment that 'there doesn't seem to be a lot of call for this type of ingredient in our general output'. The first of what would be several sessions for the ever-respected John Peel followed this rather lukewarm verdict soon afterwards. On the live circuit, in the closing weeks of 1970, they supported Roy Harper at Kingston Polytechnic and Caravan at Ewell Technical College, then played two Christmas parties—one for Charisma at the Marquee on 9 December and one on home territory back at the Rex folk club two weeks later.

Hopes were high for the group's fortunes as the new year of 1971 dawned. Charisma had the bit between their teeth as they announced two package tours for their artists, at which tickets would be priced 6s—or 30p with the advent of decimal currency a few weeks hence. The first one would feature Van der Graaf Generator, Lindisfarne, and Genesis, and the second Every Which Way, Audience, and either Jackson Heights or Rare Bird, who had given the label its first taste of chart success at the start of 1970 with the single 'Sympathy' (a Top 30 hit in Britain, but No. 1 in France and Italy). Taking a leaf out of the old package tour—which had been commonplace in the 1950s and 1960s and which would be revived by Stiff Records towards the end of the decade—it was a canny way of putting on a good value show that would break even if it sold out every hall, and go on to sell many more albums for the acts involved.

The three acts on the first tour took it in turns to top the bill on different nights, shared the same gear, and travelled together on the same tour bus. There was much camaraderie throughout, even if there was something of a difference of cultures between all of them: Genesis at the front of the vehicle with their picnics, their glasses of sherry, their *Times* crosswords, and their cameras as they eagerly snapped the more picturesque sights to be seen beyond the windows; Van der Graaf Generator at the back rolling their enormous joints; and Lindisfarne, 'rough as badgers', sitting in the middle with their crates of beer. Steve Hackett, guitarist with Genesis, called it 'three separate worlds on one coach' but found the atmosphere very friendly, regarding Jacka as the group's 'diplomat' or main contact with the outside world. As for Jacka, his memories of the tour were of a rather shy and nervous Genesis, always desperate when they went on stage for the audience to like them. Lindisfarne would be drunk, 'but that was part of their charm', and they never failed to turn in a great performance, especially of 'Lady Eleanor'.[20]

The song was becoming recognised as the highlight of their debut album as well as of their stage act, and in May, it appeared in the shops as their second single. Once again, reviews were positive and sales modest, and it narrowly failed to breach the coveted Top 50. It was said to be a favourite record of actress Tessa Wyatt, shortly to be the wife of Radio 1 presenter Tony Blackburn. Coincidentally, one of the most-played singles as the new year had begun was 'When I'm Dead and Gone', an irresistibly infectious folk-rock single written by the partnership of Benny Gallagher and Graham Lyle, both of whom were at that time part of McGuinness Flint—a group formed by ex-Manfred Mann guitarist Tom McGuinness. A record that had peaked at No. 2 over Christmas 1970 (No. 1 in some charts), it was notable not least for its prominent rhythm mandolin, played by Graham. The resemblance between this and some of Lindisfarne's goodtime sounds did not go unnoticed.

At around the same time, cover versions of both of their first two singles were released in Britain, 'Clear White Light' by Wishful Thinking and 'Lady Eleanor' by Lemon, an alias of Lem Lubin, former guitarist with Unit 4+2 and then Christie. Neither attracted much airplay or sales, but both made a faithful job of the originals.

The 'six bob tour' would always be remembered fondly by the group. Alan's abiding memory was of going to the huge Sheffield City Hall. The groups were generally used to playing either clubs or small venues, with a seating capacity of 300 or so. They walked onstage for the soundcheck, and Genesis's drummer, Phil Collins, in his 'actor' guise, suddenly appeared, looked around at the roadies, and quipped, 'That's it—gig's off. Too small!'[21]

Reviewer after reviewer fell under the spell of Lindisfarne. After the opening night of the tour at the Lyceum, London, on 24 January, Michael Wale in *The Times* called them 'entertainers in a business that at times seems intent on boring audiences to death by pomposity and "seriousness"'. To him, it seemed incredible that an audience of 1,500 southerners could be encouraged to get on their feet, clapping along to the Geordie anthem 'Blaydon Races'.[22] Moreover, the groups might not have had much in common musically, but to finish off the evening on stage, there would be a jam in which Phil Collins, Peter Hamill of Van der Graaf Generator, then Alan and Jacka each took a verse of Lonnie Donegan's 'Battle of New Orleans'.

After the tour was over, they resumed their own gigs, crisscrossing the country and playing as far afield as Belfast, Londonderry, and Glasgow, four nights in Holland, their home patch at Newcastle City Hall, various universities, and in the heart of the south-west at Torquay. There were also occasional TV appearances and further radio sessions for John Peel and Mike Raven; they joked that the radio sessions were becoming such a regular occurrence that they almost had their own coat hooks at the BBC. These broadcasts included the first performances of a new song by Rod ('Meet Me on the Corner'), an instrumental credited to all five members ('Scotch Mist'), and Alan's tongue-twisting song with singalong chorus ('Fog on the Tyne'). The latter came about because they needed something simple and rousing to finish off folk club sessions. It was a role usually taken by a rousing version of the old traditional sea shanty 'Whip Jamboree', at which punters would join in lustily and bang their glasses on the tables, so he decided he would write something of his own to take its place.

One of the most important gigs took place when they headlined at the Royal Festival Hall, London, on 10 May. With Gillian McPherson and Unicorn in the support slots, it had been arranged by Strat as a showcase for the benefit of Bob Johnston, an American staff producer for CBS Records who had overseen albums by Bob Dylan, Leonard Cohen, Johnny Cash, and Simon and Garfunkel. He was no longer bound exclusively to CBS, and it soon became common knowledge that he was planning to go into the recording studios with Lindisfarne and produce their second album.

At the gig, they decided they would feature another, more serious song by Alan—the poignant 'January Song'. It was a partial rewrite of a number that he had demoed on his own about three years earlier, 'Tomorrow—If I'm Hungry'. Some of the audience found it a little downbeat and were plainly getting restless by the end, so in order to lighten the atmosphere, they had arranged beforehand that they would follow it with 'that really daft song', using the same intro on the guitar as 'January Song', in order to fool everyone that they were about to hear another dirge. 'Fog on the Tyne', a nonsense ditty with tongue-twisting lyrics like 'sitting in a sleazy snacker sucking sickly sausage rolls', interpolating an instrumental section with Jacka on harmonica, Rod on fiddle, and Si on mandolin—plus Jacka and Si singing verses two and three respectively, Alan singing the first and last—brought the house down. Bob Johnston was among those knocked out by it, and although they had not intended it to be on the second album, it became such a favourite with audiences on successive gigs that there was no way they could leave it out.

The choice of Bob as producer was not unanimous. The entire group had reservations about John Anthony being passed over for the second album, but an opportunity to work with the same producer who had worked with several greats on the CBS label was not to be missed. Although he had as yet not been paid for 'Nicely out of Tune', John was hurt at losing out. Yet when Ray spoke to him later about it, he admitted that they would have been daft to insist on having him again when they had the chance to use Bob instead.

Their first meeting with their new producer was in a restaurant in Soho, in the company of Tony Stratton-Smith and Marty Machat, lawyer to Tony and Bob, and they found him 'larger than life, probably the first real Texan any of [them] had met'. All sessions took place at Trident Studios, Soho. For Jacka, one of the fondest memories of working there was because it had a Bösendorfer grand piano with an unmistakable sound; it was an instrument that was used on several tracks on the album and on the next record to be made there after they had finished—David Bowie's *Hunky Dory*.

Working with Bob proved to be a strange experience. The group found him a likeable character, but with a fierce side, and with his Texan accent and a peculiar way of talking, there was a definite communication problem. He disliked having his photograph taken because the Indians believed that if you did so, you would lose your spirit. When it came to recording songs to go on the album, he opted for something of a minimalist approach. The group had plenty to choose from, and had rehearsed them with plenty of lush vocal harmonies and arrangements, but in Ray's words, they had 'overdone it as far as he was concerned', and his solution was to start again. After they had played all the songs they had rehearsed and ready to record, he asked what else they had:

> We spent the rest of the day playing every song we had written, some full band, some in twos and threes and the rest as solo pieces for Alan, Rod or Si. Meanwhile Bob sat with his cowboy boots on the desk, sifting through a big bag of Mexican grass, taking the seeds out and pausing to write a yes or no next to each song title as we played it.[23]

When Roy Hollingworth, a writer on *Melody Maker*, was invited to come to the sessions one night, he was astonished to notice Bob sitting in the control booth 'with a great inane smile on his face'. During a short break, Roy asked him how he was going about producing the album. 'It's wonderful,' Bob answered, 'I just set the tape rolling and just let it go!'[24] However, after three days of recording and mixing, according to Si, he performed 'a scissors job' on the master tape, chopping choruses out, cutting verses, even songs in half. As a result of this and also his rigorous selection criteria, the end result was an album with only ten tracks and thirty-one minutes' playing time.

The album was originally to be called *Stories, Dreams and Nightmares*, but the addition of 'Fog on the Tyne', an obvious title track if ever there was one, made the decision for them. As with *Nicely out of Tune*, every song but one was an original, the exception again being another by Rab Noakes, 'Together Forever'. Of the remaining nine songs, six were written by Alan, one a collaboration with his old friend Terry Morgan, 'Peter Brophy Don't Care'. Like the title track, 'Alright On the Night' would become a regular favourite onstage with its celebratory good-time chorus, while 'City Song' and 'Passing Ghosts' were introspective, even angry numbers, almost solo performances by Alan, which shared the sombre mood of 'January Song'.

Helping to lighten the mood were Rod's two contributions, the infectious opener 'Meet Me on the Corner', and the bluesy 'Train in G Major'. Both revealed something of a Dylan influence, the former with its echoes of 'Mr Tambourine Man' and the latter 'It Takes a Lot to Laugh, It Takes a Train To Cry'. Another written by him, 'Why Can't I Be Satisfied', was recorded, but it failed to make the shortlist and would have to wait a little longer, as would three more of Alan's numbers, 'Dingly Dell', Country Gentleman's Wife', and 'Money Game'. Finally, Si made his debut as a writer with 'Uncle Sam', his sardonic comment on the Vietnam War, which he had written before the group was formed. As with Rod's songs, Jacka took the lead vocal.

'Meet Me on the Corner' had an interesting history; Jacka stated that the original version was overarranged and disjointed until he and Rod worked on it during a demo session at Covent Garden while the others went to the pub. Both of them decided to go back to the way Rod had originally recorded it on his Revox demo, as the feel of the song had been lost in the band's rearrangement. The only additions to that simple original version were harmonica, the vocal harmonies, the bass drum beat, and a small amount of piano on the chorus, which was added when the rest returned from the pub. What became known as 'the Covent Garden session demo version' was later released by accident on two compilation albums and on a reissued single after the group had split, the subtle differences between this, the album version, and the demo not being spotted by Charisma when they came to exploit the back catalogue.

One very out-of-character song, 'Who's Got The Blues, Huh?', never got as far as the starting block. It was musically closer to Frank Zappa than anything else, a song Alan had written while experimenting on electric guitar. Rod recalled one night when they opened with it at the Marquee (playing between the first two albums), Strat and John Anthony were in the audience with a look of horror on their faces. The group were eager to play rock 'n' roll as well and stretch beyond the folksy singer-songwriter template, but this first effort to break down the boundaries did not go down well and the number was abandoned there and then. Ray stated that the entire Charisma staff, led by Strat, had sharp words with them afterwards for this 'lengthy, surly, noisy, venomous song'; it was 'not the musical calling-card that Strat was hoping [they] would leave with the increasingly interested media'.[25] Rod also recalled the occasion of what may be one of the perhaps great lost Lindisfarne epics:

> Sadly, we never recorded it, even as a demo. We rehearsed it thoroughly, but didn't record rehearsals in those days. As I recall, the Marquee gig was a bit of a watershed event which didn't go well—new equipment as well as new songs (and probably a bit of a new attitude too), and we were made aware afterwards that we were in danger of losing what made us attractive in the first place. This was further driven home when Bob Johnston rejected a lot of new material on the first day of the 'Fog on the Tyne' sessions.[26]

A rather bizarre episode occurred during the session, when Alan was slightly stoned on some of Bob's California grass and ordered to follow him outside into Wardour Street. Once they were well out of earshot of the others, Bob told him that he wanted to take him over to Nashville that very night and start the whole album again 'with [his] guys'. Fortunately, Alan had the presence of mind to look into his face and say no. They then walked back through the door and the session carried on as normal. Much to his relief, Bob never brought the subject up again.

The record had been made in three or four days. Bob's approach was very different to that of John in that he used very little in the way of overdubs, just good tight live versions of the songs. According to Ray, it all sounded a little underdone to them at first, but they conceded that he knew what he was doing. It captured the very essence of the band and went on to be their biggest seller by miles. There would be no arguing with the sales figures.

After the album had been completed, Alan went back to Newcastle for a short break before the group began another tour, supporting Bell & Arc this time. Before the tour began, in a telephone interview with Roy Hollingworth, he had plenty of praise for Bob Johnston; he said Johnston had brought out things in the group that they did not realise were there before, and also referred to the possibility of a solo album as he had such a backlog of songs. He planned to go to America where he would sing Bob the lot, and he would pick them out. It would not mean the end of the group, he stressed, far from it: 'I see a formula like this as a good way to keep the band together for a fair amount of time'.[27]

The next few months were taken up with another demanding schedule of live performances, with dates at town halls up and down the land and two major festival appearances. At Reading on the last Saturday of

June, they shared the bill with East of Eden, Ralph McTell, and Wishbone Ash. Alan recalled with admiration that it was the first time Jacka 'split' the crowd: 'You 15,000 on the right—shut up. You 15,000 on the left—get your arms up in the air...' Looking at his visibly shaking front man, he said, 'Ho'way Alan, you're not nervous, are you? They're only students, man.'

Two months later, at Weeley, near Clacton-on-Sea, they were part of a line-up including The Faces, The Edgar Broughton Band, Mungo Jerry, and Rory Gallagher; they were seen by a quarter of a million, according to some estimates. Rod found the sea of people in front of them 'quite awe-inspiring', not to mention the fact that they made a habit of making the sun shine whenever they went on. Ray noted that they were evidently supplying the right element of fun at these festivals. By the time they took to the stage, audiences were beginning to suffer severe brain damage from hearing one serious prog rock outfit after another. They just took their usual slapdash, lighthearted approach. Even if there were 20,000 or more there, they would just pretend they were in a folk club and get everybody up dancing—'getting a bit of circulation in their legs after listening to someone like Caravan after four hours' worked a treat.[28]

The verdict of the music press was that The Faces and Lindisfarne were joint stars of the show. As luck would have it, there was a strong connection between the two. Jacka's mandolin playing had earned him a reputation well beyond the frontiers of the group. When The Faces' front man Rod Stewart—who had been contracted to a separate record company as a solo artist before he and Ron Wood joined The Small Faces after Steve Marriott's departure—needed such an instrument on his third album, *Every Picture Tells a Story*, he knew who to employ.

Long John Baldry, a long-time regular at the Marquee, had seen Lindisfarne there, and was so impressed with Jacka's work that he invited him to play on his next album, *It Ain't Easy*, which was being co-produced by Rod Stewart and Elton John. Rod then asked him to work on his song 'Mandolin Wind'. After the session was completed, Rod said he had another number ('Maggie May'), which needed a few more ideas. Jacka had two minutes in the studio to improvise something and instantly came up with a mandolin part to include after the final verse. As he worked it out and played it, he could see the people at the mixing desk looking at each other in delight, even applauding.

By a strange quirk of fate, Rod then played the album to friends, some of whom advised him to leave 'Maggie May' off as it had no tune and was the worst track of the lot, but he kept it all the same. When his version of Tim Hardin's 'Reason to Believe' was chosen as a single on both sides of the Atlantic, 'Maggie May' went on the B-side. After several weeks of airplay for the former, a radio DJ in Milwaukee turned it over and began playing 'Maggie' instead. One or two television appearances for Rod and The Faces and their appearance at Weeley boosted the record into the British Top 50. Within a fortnight, 'Maggie' had displaced 'Reason' as the A-side; by the end of September, it was at No. 1 in Britain, staying there for five weeks, repeating its success in America and also sending the album to the summit on both sides of the Atlantic. It was something that nobody else, not even The Beatles at their peak, had ever achieved with the same single and album. Jacka's reward for his part in this success was £15, the standard Musicians' Union fee for a three-hour session.

Ironically, the back of the Rod Stewart album sleeve carried a credit for 'the mandolin player in Lindisfarne', whose name apparently escaped his memory. He was a little more generous in his memoirs some forty years later, as Jacka would wryly acknowledge on stage: '[it was] a nice mandolin part, played by Ray Jackson from the folk-rock group Lindisfarne—and you don't often hear mandolin on a pop song'.[29] Rod's appearances on *Top of the Pops* featured him singing a live vocal, with The Faces miming to the backing track and kicking a football around in the TV studio, while presenter John Peel—invited on as he had been an ardent champion of the group on his Radio 1 show—nervously mimed the mandolin part, having been assured by the Musicians' Union that to do so was permissible as long as he was not seen to make any effort to play the instrument. Such a combination of circumstances made Jacka the most renowned unknown mandolin player in the business, to say nothing of fuelling a rumour that John had actually been on the record. Though not pleased at such cavalier treatment, Jacka also played mandolin on Rod's two subsequent chart-topping solo albums, *Never A Dull Moment* and *Smiler*. The single from the latter, 'Farewell', reached No. 7 in October 1974.

In between festivals and sessions, the gigs kept on coming. On 11 September, there were two: a long-scheduled booking at Salisbury and, earlier that day, a spot in an all-day affair at the Oval Cricket Ground, Kennington. With The Who headlining, Rod Stewart and The Faces and Mott the Hoople also on the bill, it was staged in aid of the Bangladesh famine victims, hot on the heels of the first major charity concert staged for the same cause by George Harrison, Ravi Shankar, and friends in New York the previous month. Everything was going Lindisfarne's way. Later, in September, *Melody Maker* published its annual readers' poll, placing them runners-up in the Brightest British New Hope category, behind Wishbone Ash, and seventh in the International section.

When advance copies of *Fog on the Tyne* were sent to the music press, the reviews were unfailingly generous. *Disc & Music Echo* cited it as evidence that they were 'the most original British group of the past two years', remarking that the group were so closely knit that it was impossible to spot the individual writers, while *Sounds* called it 'an absolute master conception'. In *New Musical Express*, Roy Carr singled Jacka out for special praise, noting that he did a mean vocal and was also one of the most original instrumentalists to have emerged in the last couple of years. Alan readily acknowledged Jacka's importance in the group—as the best singer and the link between them and the audience—saying that if anyone left Lindisfarne, they would 'die completely, and never be reborn'. Not for another year would that judgment be put to the test.

3

'All Fall Down'

Fog on the Tyne was released in October 1971. In Newcastle, two record shops placed orders for 3,000 copies between them and sold over 300 on the first day. As a thank you to local fans, the group made a personal appearance in one shop and were mobbed in the street. At last they had a national hit on their hands when the record entered the album chart at No. 23. Demand was thus fuelled for the year-old *Nicely Out of Tune*, which made a long-overdue album chart debut a couple of months later and stayed there for thirty weeks.

Lindisfarne really were the flavour of the month. After a gig at the Brighton Dome, an enthusiastic crowd rose to its feet and started dancing not only in the aisles but also on stage. Afterwards, Strat was curtly informed by the management that no more concerts featuring artists signed to Charisma would be staged at the venue. When he responded in the media, bemoaning about old-fashioned attitudes on the part of people being out of touch with today's music business, a spokesman responded that the ban would not apply to other artists, only to Lindisfarne, because they had 'behaved in a really unruly way', encouraging the audience to jump on stage with them.

The reception was more friendly at most other venues, not least of all their native Newcastle, where they were treated like conquering heroes returning home at a concert on 4 December—a pre-Christmas party complete with balloons and paper hats. A forerunner of an event that later became something of an annual tradition, it was recorded by the BBC for a television documentary to be screened in the new year. By this time, some of the songs had undergone slight changes since being committed to vinyl. An extended 'Clear White Light' was given a Bo Diddley beat and integrated a brief snatch of 'Not Fade Away'. 'Alright On the Night', the second track from *Fog on the Tyne*, had been given an almost reggae beat as they were 'fed up with doing lovely little folk songs', a point presumably not lost on Jamaican reggae act The Pioneers, who were currently at the

peak of their British chart success and went on to record their own version
on the album *I Believe In Love* the following year. Most notably of all,
'We Can Swing Together' now lasted around fifteen minutes, with an
extended middle section featuring Jacka's harmonica medley that might
include anything from sea shanties and folk tunes to 'Mademoiselle
From Armentieres' and the theme from the long-running BBC drama
series *Z Cars*. Supporting them at the concert were Rab Noakes and
Stealers Wheel.

For a while, the group could seemingly do no wrong. Alan was full
of praise for the fans in Newcastle who had supported them, but less
charitable to the groups in London that he said were born with silver
spoons in their mouths: 'We were born with pickaxes in ours and we spat
them right out at them'. It took a journalist from *Northern Correspondent*
some years later to point out politely that Alan's bandmates Rod and Si
had been educated at fee-paying Kings' School in Tynemouth and might
not have appreciated the comment.[1] For a while, he revelled in The Beatles
comparisons, saying he wanted Lindisfarne to be as big as they were; it
was pointless 'having ambition if you don't aim to be the best', and in
about two years' time, he honestly believed they would produce an album
of the standard of *Abbey Road*. John Lennon was mentioned as a great
songwriter in the same breath as Bob Dylan and Robbie Robertson: 'All
their work reflects something that is totally real'.[2]

Although the group were not chasing singles success, it was inevitable
that the need for some attention to the 45-rpm market would follow.
During the same week that the album was released, they went into Island
Studios, again with Bob Johnston as producer. They recorded another
version of Alan's song (which had originally been tried out a few weeks
earlier but was scrapped) and a harmonica-and-fiddle-led instrumental,
'Scotch Mist', written by Jacka although credited jointly to all five as
writers. 'No Time to Lose' had originally been meant for a film, *Some Kind
of Hero*. Strat was keen to diversify into motion pictures, but this idea of
his, a drama centred around a Vietnam draft dodger and his girlfriend in
Britain, proved an ambition too far. Another song by Alan was written
around the title of the as-yet unmade epic, but neither song nor film ever
saw the light of day.

With their heavy gigging schedule, it was clear that something had to
give. By the end of the year, all five exhausted members were swearing that
they would never work as hard as this again. Si stated: '[It was] killing the
magic. And it's not doing us much good either'.[3] They did not have enough
time to come up with new material, yet they could not rest on their laurels
because the third album was going to have to be the one to end all albums.

Luckily, they were given a breathing space when it came to the next release. When *Fog on the Tyne* hit the shops, they had no plans to take any tracks off as a single. That all changed in the first week of February 1972, when the infectious 'Meet Me on the Corner', which had proved an instant success on stage, appeared on the A-side, backed by 'No Time to Lose' and 'Scotch Mist'. It was a time when some groups and their management, notably the Led Zeppelins of the industry, regarded singles as being for the younger and less discerning or affluent consumers, although other acts appreciated the importance of a hit 45 as strategic marketing, a way to sell more albums. Rod Stewart might not have been propelled into the musical first division had 'Maggie May' just remained as an album track.

Alan was a much more prolific writer than Rod, as the latter readily admitted: '[He was] quite competitive too. I think it always irked him a bit that 'Meet Me on the Corner' was the first hit—he never let me forget it'.[4] The song received a Certificate of Honour at the Ivor Novello Awards that year. In America, a more countrified version by Henry Gross had minor success as a single, while in 1975, ''39', a track on Queen's *A Night at the Opera* and easily the most folksy sounding track in their catalogue, was said to have been influenced more than a little by the song.

In general, the group were unimpressed with much of the charts. Ray stated that, five years previously, before albums had reached their early 1970s level, acts really used their imagination to make a good record:

> But apart from consistently good groups like The Move, most of the material we hear now is pure rubbish. Half the records played on the radio aren't even worth the plastic they are printed on. They must be fools not to realise that by lowering the standards they are cutting their own throats.[5]

Jacka admitted that chasing singles success might possibly work against them. They had no desire to become another T. Rex, but he did not see much danger of that. 'Meet Me on the Corner' was 'an album track after all and not a deliberate sell-out single'.[6]

Regular airplay on Radio 1 followed, as did appearances on *Top of the Pops,* with Alan sporting a Russian army uniform from the BBC props department and Ray banging his drums with a rubber fish. He said that had been inspired partly by the drum sound Levon Helm of The Band used to get: 'A flat, slappy sound like he was hitting it with a herring. So I said to our manager get me a rubber fish so I can get that sound too!' As for appearing on television's only chart show of the time, they did not share the distaste for it that some of their peers did, and entered wholeheartedly into the fun of being on the show:

More people remember me for hitting my drum kit with a rubber fish than anything else I've ever done. But *Top of the Pops* was a great shop front for us. Everybody watched that show in those days. And because you mimed, you could have a drink too and it didn't matter if you got drunk.[7]

With what might have seemed less than perfect timing, the hit coincided with their debut in America. Their last date in Britain for several weeks was at the Queen Elizabeth Hall, London, at which they played two new songs by Alan. 'Mandolin King' was uncontroversial enough, but the heartfelt 'Poor Old Ireland' ('Poor old Ireland, poor old universe, wonder which comes off the worst') was banned by the BBC when it appeared on album later that year. Two singles released at around that time, Wings' self-explanatory 'Give Ireland Back to the Irish', and McGuinness Flint's 'Let the People Go', with a lyric protesting about internment in Northern Ireland, were also excluded from airplay, with the former being referred to on air during Radio 1 chart rundowns as 'a record by Wings'.

Lindisfarne's next appearances on stage were at Carnegie Hall, New York, where they were supporting The Kinks on 2 and 3 March. At an after-gig party, members of both groups had a spontaneous singalong, in which they were joined by Leslie West of Mountain. They had been provisionally booked to do ten days, but it 'just snowballed' and they ended up staying and performing for eight weeks. Dates were arranged along the east coast and west coast with The Beach Boys. 'We hung out at The Troubador in LA where Jackson Browne and The Eagles used to hang out and we supported Don McLean there,' said Ray. As a lifelong fan of The Kinks in particular, he found it appropriate that Lindisfarne should be playing dates with them as both groups attracted the kind of audience who were interested in songs rather than instrumental virtuosity. He relished the experience and found the tour 'wonderful'.

Press reviews were good, though there had been some concern as to how an act whose presentation relied a good deal on humour from the north-east of England would fare on the other side of the Atlantic. One reviewer opined that for all their positive qualities, the group lacked discipline and would do well to 'forget their easygoing Geordie heritage and cut out the sloppiness'. Too much chat onstage about Tyneside, brown ale, and Magpies (Newcastle United) FC was fine at home, but meant nothing to anybody elsewhere. However, as Alan pointed out, 'you don't stop being who you are just because you happen to be in New York'.[8]

On successive dates, they played as support act to the likes of Tim Buckley and Taj Mahal, but it was hard work and their reception could be mixed. Part of the problem, they felt, was that Elektra, the label to which they were signed in America, did not seem particularly interested in promoting them. Nevertheless, their meteoric rise continued on the other side of the Atlantic. In the last week of March, 'Meet Me on the Corner' reached its peak position of No. 5, while after going up and down the album chart for five months and occasionally disappearing completely, *Fog on the Tyne* had reached No. 1 and would stay there for four weeks; *Nicely out of Tune* had also belatedly climbed into the Top 20. There were champagne celebrations at the Charisma office in London, they learned, so on the other side of the Atlantic, the group clubbed their small change together for a bottle of Californian wine.

Strat laid on a generous reception for them when they returned to England, even though it was only a short break before the round of more and more gigs started again. Ray stated that when they were back on their home territory, they had three weeks of being famous and not being able to walk the streets in Newcastle without being mobbed: 'We didn't have minders or anything like that. It was all very good-natured but you still couldn't escape from it. We loved every minute but then I went back to North Shields and no one took any notice of me there!'[9] Rod recalled the experience in much the same way, considering it 'a dream come true for five simple Geordie lads'. They returned to Newcastle from the States when they were at No. 1, did an album signing at one major local shop, Windows in the Arcade, and they were mobbed: 'It lasted a couple of weeks then it was back down to earth with a bump—but they were great days.'[10]

Early in the summer, there was a new lease of life for the previous single 'Lady Eleanor', which was reactivated after radio DJs expressed interest. After generous airplay and further appearances on *Top of the Pops*, in June it reached No. 3, the same week that *Nicely out of Tune* sold enough to reach its highest position of No. 8; Alan was astonished by its success:

> I wrote it almost in a trance and I know it means something, personal to me, and it would take a long time to explain—I know it's about death anyway, and I'm very worried about it being a so-called hit because I'm worried about the 17 and 16-year-old girls and boys who buy it. I mean it's not a pop song and I don't understand what they think about it.... I think the kids just take the songs as they find them, maybe it's just the sound that they like. With 'Lady Eleanor' I'm worried in the sense that I don't understand, and I'm always worried about things that I don't understand—I just wanna know what they get out of it. I mean I can understand what they get out of T. Rex, because it's sex, and that's fine, and I can understand what they get out of a good pop song; but I put 'Lady Eleanor' in the same category as 'A Whiter Shade of Pale' by

Procol Harum—I don't know why people bought that in their thousands because it's a very mystical song.[11]

Lindisfarne were among the acts who played on the main stage at the four-day Lincoln Festival on Sunday 28 May, alongside Slade, The Beach Boys, and Monty Python's Flying Circus—the comedy act who also recorded for Charisma. During an abnormally cold and wet early summer, the group put on what was acclaimed as one of the best performances there, though not even they could save the organisers Great Western Festivals Ltd from losing an estimated £200,000 on the event.

By now, Lindisfarne saw themselves moving gently from the folk genre into a more rock-based direction. Rod explained that they had always been more folksy on the albums and much rockier on stage because the latter was more exciting for the audience to watch and for the musicians to play:

> The reason that we got into folk is that the songs are uppermost and we are a writing band. We've always been looking round for a form to express our songs best without instrumental indulgences and we're still going to play songs as songs, it's just that they'll be rock songs rather than folk. Actually it's not a question of writing different sorts of songs, it's really the way we play them. We would have done all right as a folk band because of our songs, but it's a question of doing what we want to do. For me being a bass player automatically means that I'm used to rhythm sections, amplifiers, funkiness and all the rest.[12]

Songwriting was, as always, of the essence, but it was perfectly possible to combine the two musical genres. There were many groups around, he maintained, who were good rock and rollers, but indifferent songwriters, with the prominent exception of The Rolling Stones:

> I think *Sticky Fingers* was excellent music, from a rock and roll and lyrical point of view. The kind of thing that Dylan started with words hasn't been followed up really. I've just been listening to *Highway 61* [*Revisited*] a lot again and it's shit hot musically and the words are miles in advance of anyone else. 'Lady Eleanor' wasn't a heavy song in the *Highway 61* or *Sticky Fingers* sense but I think it tells a story in an intelligent sort of way that people can get something out of.[13]

Despite having had two Top 5 singles and appeared on *Top of the Pops*, he emphasised that they were in no hurry to issue another. As far as they were concerned, it was a trap into which they did not wish to fall. In their view, it was fine to issue certain tracks thus if they seemed marketable. He was sure there would be more singles, but they had nothing in mind at the time.

That summer, it was time for the outfit recognised as Britain's biggest-selling albums act to give serious thought as to what would be on their third long player. Another round of gigs, among them a very well-received show at Queen's Hall, Barnstaple, on 7 July, gave them a chance to try out some of the newer songs on stage before they went into Island Studios for four days of recording from 14 to 17 July. They had had little time or energy in recent months to pen fresh material, but there was still a healthy backlist of songs to draw upon.

By way of contrast to the previous sessions at Trident for the second album, this time the group had decided for themselves which songs they wanted to use and worked everything out beforehand. In Rod's words, it was more a matter of 'direct, whack-it-down, almost like playing live'. Bob Johnston was more laid-back and less in control this time, making rather unhelpful remarks to them along the lines of having better places to be—like the Caribbean. He let the engineer, Bob Potter, get on with it as the group played one song after another, while he did little more than sit there and suggest one or two ideas when it came to the mixing. On one hand, it did not give them a great deal of confidence, but on the other hand, the group had or at least exuded the attitude that whatever they did would be a success. *New Musical Express* noted sagely that they were the darlings of show business without a cloud on the horizon, and if it was possible to kill a group with kindness, then they might be the victims of their own success. Hopes were high all around as Alan talked of striving for perfection and creating a brilliant album to stand alongside *Sergeant Pepper* or *Abbey Road*.[14]

Eight of the twelve tracks on *Dingly Dell* had been written by Alan. In addition to 'Mandolin King' and 'Poor Old Ireland', there was 'All Fall Down'. This was a song in which an exquisite tune and arrangement of strings and brass could not conceal a bitter diatribe against the iniquities of city planners and their contempt for their heritage and the environment, decimating the city centre with a motorway ('who needs the trees and the flowers to grow—we can have a motorway with motorway dough'), and the self-explanatory 'Bring Down the Government'. The guitar riff in the latter song had been 'borrowed' from an old Joe Brown song, and there was some mild embarrassment when Joe arrived at the Charisma offices on business while somebody was playing the track. The title track was a brooding, almost ambient six-minute number about a woodland, where, he said, he used to take his small daughters hunting for hobbits. Delivering some swooping lines on fretless bass, Rod was the only member of the group to accompany Alan on the song, supplemented (like 'All Fall Down') by a string arrangement from Ray's brother Paul. However, to balance the lyrically deeper and the less commercial fare was one of Alan's most joyous, uncomplicated pop numbers ever, 'Wake Up Little Sister', and a lively rock 'n' roll tune with a riff that tipped its hat to Eddie Cochran, 'Court in the Act'. Elsewhere on the album, Si contributed a quirky instrumental, 'Plankton Lament', and the infectious 'Go Back'. Rod's contribution was 'Don't Ask Me', a dark number with a sardonic lyric on the nature of success and pop stardom, with a biting guitar riff and slide guitar that emphasised his leaning towards pure rock territory.

When the album was completed, a preview was held for the press and various friends, including Jacka's fiancée Karen and Rab Noakes. The media reaction was upbeat, the general verdict being that the group's style had matured and was moving slightly away from folk. One reviewer added that it was as well The Beatles were no longer recording because they would now have serious rivals. Could there be any higher praise?

Although only the group and those closest to them were aware, the album for which critics had fallen over themselves in finding the right words had had a troubled birth. When they received the master pressing, they were dissatisfied with the sound. In particular, Rod was horrified to hear no proper bass on it, even after much tweaking. When Barbara Hayes came around to his house one day, he insisted to her that they could not release it in its present form. After they listened to it together, she told him she could not hear anything wrong, and to prove his point, he played her an album by Leon Russell—and the bass came pounding out. That, he told her, was what records were meant to sound like. 'Yes, but that's not folk, dear,' was her reaction.[15] Yet Lindisfarne were not simply a folk outfit, and remix it they did.

Having put that behind them, still riding the crest of a wave, they played the Crystal Palace Garden Party on 2 September alongside Yes, the Mahavishnu Orchestra, and fellow Charisma signing Capability Brown. On 3 October, they began a twenty-date tour, sharing a bill with Genesis and Rab Noakes, starting at Sheffield and finishing on 29 October at Lewisham.

It was at around this point that things started to go wrong. The reason was a combination of several factors. One was that of a group who felt they could do no wrong, say anything they liked, try out new ideas, and expect the world to beat a path to their door. The other was that of a media which revelled in the build-'em up, knock-'em down syndrome. Today's darlings could easily be tomorrow's has-beens. They were about to become victims of their own success, something they could not sustain. In the summer of 1972, the group was extremely popular, and consequently when their honeymoon with the music press came to an end, it hit them hard.

Ray stated that *Dingly Dell* always remained their most underrated album. He thought it was a big step forward from the previous two albums, on which nearly all the songs they recorded had been written prior to the group being successful. This time, apart from the title track, the material was all new. It was also the second album with Bob Johnston as producer, they played more confidently in the studio, and the subject matter and instrumentation of the new songs took them along some different paths.

There were three reasons why it ultimately turned into such a disappointment. Firstly, 'All Fall Down' had been released as a single in mid-September, backed with a seven-minute edit from the live version of 'We Can Swing Together'. Nearly everyone had been convinced that the new 45 would be 'Wake Up Little Sister', and none more than Noddy Holder of Slade, who was convinced that it would have been number one when Wolverhampton's favourite four were aiming for yet another chart topper.[16] Instead, they had chosen a song which in its own way was just as good, but too serious. Songs about how Newcastle City planners and developers were desecrating the man in the street's pride and joy were not 'radio'. Joni Mitchell's 'Big Yellow Taxi' with its refrain of 'they paved paradise and put up a parking lot' had narrowly missed the Top 10 two years earlier, but there is one exception to every rule. 'All Fall Down' limped to No. 34 and soon fell from sight. Ray later admitted that it had been a marketing failure, and had they got that all-important first single right, a radio audience and record-buying public would have accepted the lyrically heavier material after that.[17]

'Court in the Act' was the follow-up single a couple of months later and died a death as far as airplay and sales went. Capability Brown, another group signed to Charisma, had recorded 'Wake Up Little Sister' with a more prominent guitar riff. When Lindisfarne dug their heels in for 'All Fall Down', the label released Brown's version as a 45, but despite regular plays on Radio Luxembourg, it also failed to chart. In spite of this setback, the group also recorded another of Alan's songs, 'I Am and So Are You', on their subsequent album *Voice*. There was another connection in that two members of the group had previously been with Harmony Grass, a briefly successful 1960s outfit that had evolved from Tony Rivers and the Castaways. Tony, who was in the line-up of both earlier names, later became a session singer and was the voice on the anonymous cover version of 'Lady Eleanor', which appeared on a *Top of the Pops* budget price album on the Hallmark label in 1972.

The packaging of *Dingly Dell* was also a brave gesture, and a monumental *faux pas* at the same time. Its plain drab recycled cardboard sleeve was 'an anti-packaging idea', with only the group name and title on the outside, plus an inner bag with full track-by-track credits and a large sepia poster. When Charisma told them they were making a mistake, they refused to change their minds. The result was an almost invisible record that sold to the committed fan, but barely merited more than a cursory glance from the average punter in the high street, when a conspicuous sleeve would scream 'buy me!'

Ray could remember 'Wake Up Little Sister' being suggested as the first single from the album:

> Although we realised how commercial it could have been we were in the midst of an ecologically aware/anti-commercialism phase, the raw grey cardboard cover of *Dingly Dell* was another manifestation of this. We felt that 'All Fall Down' was making a statement. To be honest we overestimated our status as eco-warriors and the combination of a dreary sleeve and a protest song in an alternating 6/8 and 3/4 time signature dissipated the excitement around our third album. If 'Wake Up Little Sister' had been the first single I'm sure it would have been a much bigger success and the resulting higher album sales would have delivered our message to loads more people.[18]

Possibly the most important factor was that *Fog on the Tyne* had been the right record in the right place at the right time, a huge seller beyond anybody's wildest dreams. *Dingly Dell*, the group was convinced, was a better record and would therefore sell even better. Nobody at Charisma pointed out that such a phenomenal achievement would be well-nigh impossible to repeat, and that it was unlikely that any subsequent album, no matter how brilliant, would have the same success.

Once press copies were sent out, reviewers gave it a mixed reception. Some praised it, while others gave it a thumbs down. A number of journalists who loved it at the preview a few weeks earlier, one imagines, had not received a copy as the brickbats came in. One said he had tried hard to be objective, but he found it really limp, with the songs, vocals, and playing 'so utterly devoid of feeling'. Initial sales were strong, and it entered the charts at No. 5, staying in the Top 10 for five weeks, only to fall out of the Top 50 by the end of the year after ten weeks (the first two albums had lasted twenty-six and fifty-six weeks respectively). Alan was quick to put his finger on the reason:

> We didn't capitalise or consolidate the success we had right then. We were right at the top and we blew it. It was as simple as that. We blew it. We just went into the studio with the attitude whatever we do is going to

be good because we're good. And whatever we do is going to sell because we're popular. That's the wrong attitude to go into the studio with—as we've since found out.[19]

Shortly before they had gone into the studios in July, Rod had said that the third album was the one that traditionally gets knocked after the first two have been praised. He probably never spoke a truer word.[20]

In retrospect, the album has been acknowledged as far from the artistic disaster that it was close to being dubbed, but that was not how it seemed at the time. About a month after release to primarily very good reviews, said Ray, it was considered a flop:

When I listen to *Dingly Dell* now, I don't feel the bad vibes that used to be associated with it. It sounds fresh, optimistic and very musical; it's a shame that a great album became the innocent victim of the band's inexperience and our management's lack of balls by giving in when we spat our dummies out.[21]

The accompanying tour was by no means a failure, but they were clearly no longer flavour of the month in the music press. The relative disappointment of the album's reception dogged the group, made them unsure of themselves, and put them in some doubt as to their next move. They admitted to being nervous and feeling unsettled about the new material, and in turn, this impacted on the response from audiences. A review in *Melody Maker* of one gig referred to their performance as 'wooden'.

Towards the end of the year, they scooped healthy places in the music weeklies' readers' polls, particularly when 'Lady Eleanor' was voted the Best British Single of 1972 in *Melody Maker*. Even so, it was a subdued group who returned to America in November. Within a few days of their arrival, they played several dates, including one supporting the Beach Boys and another with David Bowie, whose star was currently ascending following the success of his *Ziggy Stardust* album. Another, on which they would have been supporting their hero Frank Zappa, failed to materialise when he did a Ginger Baker and refused to move his gear so they could set up their equipment to play. Long travel between gigs, much of it in two station wagons with members split between the two, did nothing for the group camaraderie.

Although the tour coincided with the height of glam rock, Lindisfarne refused to bow to sartorial trends. Alan in particular kept doggedly to his denim shirt and jeans onstage. On one occasion, he borrowed a more flamboyant shirt from one of the management, and threw it in to the audience. Only later did he realise that the pocket had contained a three-figure sum in banknotes.[22]

They returned to Britain for Christmas and enjoyed some brief breathing space before flying to Germany for five dates in January, followed by a tour of Australia with Slade, Status Quo, and Caravan. Yet morale was still at a low ebb. Alan disliked being on the road so much, partly because the travel was making it impossible for him to write new songs, something he could really only do with ease sitting at home, and partly because he was missing his wife and three daughters badly. Rod was the only other one with a wife and family, while the other three had no such ties and were happy to make the most of it before settling down. The general dissatisfaction with their lot spread, with heated conversations between two or three at a time, instead of a full group brainstorming session that would have probably resolved any issues and cleared the air at once.

Alan's bitterness with Charisma came to the surface as he lambasted those who were getting their 10–15 per cent sitting in an office in London while they were on the other side of the world, doing all the hard work, getting on and off planes and concert stages. Everyone at the company was keen for the group to carry on regardless, mainly because their earnings were keeping the label and company afloat. However, his main objective was for some badly needed time off the road, so he could rekindle his songwriting muse.

A few months earlier, Si had identified the problem and the lack of a conducive atmosphere to writing new material for all of them:

> Alan would sit in his Gateshead pad and sing five songs straight out of his head and we'd do them the next day. He's written about three songs since then and that's about one and a half years ago. We came to London and there's such a heavy blanket covering the place I don't think we've ever managed to settle in.[23]

Some of them felt they should return to America for another period of intensive touring to establish themselves properly there. The only factor they had not considered and probably should have was getting new management, renegotiating their contract, taking some time off to think, write, and rehearse, and then return with their batteries fully recharged. That was exactly what Genesis did about a year later.

Strat's solution was for Alan to take on a non-performing relationship with the group, similar to that of Brian Wilson with The Beach Boys, whereby he would write for and record with them but not go out on the road. It dovetailed with Alan's own idea, as he had suggested to the others that he rather liked the idea of being a part-time member. His place on stage could be taken by their friend from way back, Billy 'Mitch' Mitchell, whose voice and rhythm guitar work would fill the gap perfectly. Although the others respected Billy as a performer, they were less taken with the idea of Alan stepping back in such a way. As a compromise, Rod suggested that they should take time off, mainly to give him a chance to write new material without the pressure that was making his role as their main songwriter impossible.

Meanwhile, the tour on the other side of the world had its good, not so good, and its unforeseen moments. On one of their days off in Australia, all the groups were treated to a tour of McKinley's champagne factory, and on the way back, there was a roof-raising singsong at which Jacka and Noddy Holder vied with each other to be the life and soul of the party. At the next gig the following day, both vocalists realised they had paid the price—the both of them could barely sing. Then there was mayhem on what had promised to be a long and tedious 7,000-mile flight from Perth to Sydney, enlivened by a fight involving sausage rolls, pies, and custard, and one member of Status Quo removing his clothes. It led to a mass arrest when they landed at Perth, getting banged up and told to behave themselves in future on release, plus a lifelong ban from Australian Airlines for the most guilty. Last but not least, there was also the little matter of Rod and Si checking into their hotel room in Melbourne, discovering to their delight a suite full of crates of champagne and every other drink imaginable, making the most of it—then learning only too late that they had just consumed everybody's supply that was meant to last all five of them for the whole tour.

After the dates in Australia and New Zealand, Lindisfarne flew to Japan for gigs on their own. On Valentine's Day, they played what would be their final gig together—for the next few years—at Shibuya Public Hall, Tokyo. Afterwards, an exhausted and short-tempered Alan swore at Si, telling him he was not going to have him in the group anymore because he was always tuning up on stage. Si was a perfectionist, and the accusation was not a completely unfair one, but such dedication to his craft hardly amounted to an instant sacking offence. Rod and Ray felt that to blame Si for their problems was not only unfair but ridiculous, with Rod making the point that they had so many guitars in different tunings that they lost a lot of pace on gigs. All of them needed to tighten up their on-stage behaviour as they had become a little unprofessional, and Alan was no exception. If Si had to go, vowed Rod and Ray, they would too.

Feelings had been running high for a while and angry words were exchanged all around, with members splitting roughly into two camps. There was a strong affinity between Si, Rod, and Ray, all of whom initially saw Jacka as torn between staying with them and remaining with Alan.

Jacka felt he was at odds with Rod and Si over the choice of new material and general musical direction. Ever the mediator between both factions, Ray was undecided until it was evident that the group was going to split in two, when he chose to remain with Rod and Si. Some kind of division was inevitable, for as Alan later admitted, if they had tried to carry on as before, they would soon have become enemies.

Everybody agreed that it was no longer fun. It was a no-win situation, and many years afterwards, Ray said he believed that with the benefit of hindsight they had been rather naïve. Despite their internal differences, which invariably always reared their head with any group sooner or later, the name Lindisfarne 'had a hell of a lot going for it'. Had they stuck it out, he was sure they could have eventually resolved any issues and gone on to build on what had on balance been a very promising start in the USA, which would, if given time, have turned them into a huge international success:

> [The initial solution that had been suggested by Alan was] very unfair and Rod and I couldn't have gone along with it so rather than get into protracted negotiations we jumped ship and probably waved goodbye to a lot of money.[24]

With his vast backlog of songs, it had long been Alan's intention to record a solo album at some stage, though not under Bob Johnston's auspices in Nashville. With the group now facing an uncertain future, there was no better time. The result, *Pipedream*, was laid down in sessions taking just over a week, from 19 to 27 March, Jacka contributing harmonica and mandolin and Ray drums. He said:

> [He and Alan] had a perfectly cordial relationship about everything other than his remedy for the band's ills and when he asked me to play on the *Pipedream* sessions I had no hesitation in accepting. I'm glad I did, we had a ball and made a great record.[25]

The other musicians were friends with whom Alan had planned to work for a while. They included Kenny Craddock (a keyboard player and guitarist, who had been in local group The Elcort and had also been a guest musician on their Newcastle Christmas concert in 1971), guitarist Johnny Turnbull and Colin Gibson (former members of The Chosen Few), and then Skip Bifferty. For a co-producer, he turned to another old friend from Newcastle, Mickey Sweeney. Two songs on the album, 'Money Game' and 'Country Gentleman's Wife', had initially been recorded and then rejected during the *Fog on the Tyne* sessions. 'United States of Mind' had been played live on the last British tour, while 'Drug Song', written during his nursing days, first saw the light of day as part of a Radio 1 session for Bob Harris.

Pipedream was the album that Alan had always wanted to make. Critics and admirers would choose it as arguably the peak of his artistic career, with a warmth and humanity that combined several of the themes on which he often dealt so articulately. Among them were his contempt for business, despite (like so many other professional musicians the world over) being inescapably part of it, as well as romance, family life, and class differences. Always an enthusiastic champion of Alan's work, Roy Hollingworth wrote in *Melody Maker* that eleven of the twelve songs were nothing short of brilliant (one track, 'STD 0632', named after the Newcastle dialling code, was an instrumental, not a song), and that overall it was 'a lot prettier and softer' than the music he was famous for—though at the same time there was 'also an air of the sinister'.

Two tracks were released as singles, the gently ironic 'Justanothersadsong' and the more autobiographical 'Numbers (Travelling Band)'. The latter was about the boredom of the first tour, when they, Genesis, and Van der Graaf Generator shared a bus the length and breadth of the country, losing most of what money they had earned as stars in the making on card and domino games played in the back of the bus. The adulterous story of 'Country Gentleman's Wife' was inspired by his window-cleaning days in the more affluent areas of Newcastle, although he stressed that the situation described in the lyrics never actually arose.

His own personal favourite from the album was 'Drug Song', which he had penned on the same night as 'Clear White Light'. He stated that they were the only two songs he had ever written completely under the influence: 'And I thought, "what am I doing to myself?" and I was writing this tune'. When pressed to say whether it was anti-drugs, he remained equivocal, admitting that it had a slight bias against them:

> I don't believe in saying things definitely. It's not my philosophy. You can say what you think a thing is, but you can't say it's either bad or good. I just don't like a philosophy of directness … complete yes or no.[26]

A section inside the gatefold sleeve of the album presented a gallery of shots—some clearly out of focus—of his wife, children, friends, and fellow musicians. The front featured a painting, *La Lampe Philosophique*, by Belgian surrealist artist René Magritte, but only after negotiations with the artist's estate, which cost Charisma a fee of £4,000. Alan had long since been fascinated by surrealism in general and Magritte in particular, and the same picture would adorn the front cover of a sixty-four-page paperback, *Mocking Horse*; this was a collection of thirty-seven of Alan's poems written over the previous ten years, published by Charisma under the imprint of Spice Box Books that summer. At the front was a dedication to 'all the nurses of St Nicholas's Hospital and all the nurses all over the world'. The original cover price was 75p, but forty years later, the never-reprinted volume had become a rare collector's item with even worn, well-used copies being offered for sums many times its original value.

Alan seemed rather more modest about his poetical abilities than his songwriting prowess. When broached on the subject of his book, he seemed less sure of himself, telling Strat that he was 'welcome but daft' when the latter told him he ought to publish. He considered himself to be a songwriter:

> I'm not the best in the world, but I know I can do it. However, there are people who spend their lives writing poetry and songwriting is the difference between fine art and graphic art. I don't know why I write them. I think I'm crackers.

Adding that he had originally wanted to call the book *Read This When You're Drunk!*, he referred to his poems as 'the ravings of a drunken, deranged mind'.[27] Unlike Leonard Cohen, who was at one time almost as well-known for his published verse as his songs, going into print was not an experience Alan would repeat in the future. Music remained his main vocation, and a new chapter was about to open.

'Taking Care of Business'

A month after *Pipedream* was completed, it was officially confirmed that Lindisfarne would split, but not disband completely. Rod, Si, and Ray were in the process of forming a new group under a different name with Billy, while Alan and Jacka, as the front men of the old group, would be recruiting new musicians and retaining the name of Lindisfarne.

Following the sessions for the solo album, Alan planned to keep what he called the Pipedream group together. Alan Hull's Pipedream—his intention being to give them a new name—would thus also comprise Jacka, Ray, Kenny Craddock, Johnny Turnbull, and Colin Gibson. To his disappointment, and that of Jacka as well, Ray confirmed that after some consideration, he was going to stay with the other two. In order to fill the drum stool, Alan then turned to Phil Collins. They had been friendly since the 'six bob tour' days, and as Genesis were currently doing what Lindisfarne should have done and were taking a sabbatical, he was keeping his hand in with a scratch band. Jacka had seen them playing at a pub in West Kensington and was impressed with their more jazzy style. As he and Alan were looking towards taking the music in a different direction, they decided that he would be just right for what they had in mind. After a generously alcohol-fuelled meeting in the pub one evening, Phil was almost persuaded to join them, but said he needed to run it past Strat before making up his mind, and he would ring them later. Loath to have not one, but two of his star acts splitting or at least undergoing major personnel changes, Strat advised Phil to stay with Genesis, who he was sure would hit the big time sooner or later. When Phil phoned Alan back to decline his offer, he was warned, 'You'll regret this decision for the rest of your life.'[1]

Colin and Johnny likewise had other commitments, the latter as he had just begun working with the promising though yet unknown Ian Dury. At length, the second Lindisfarne line-up was confirmed with Alan, Jacka, and Kenny being joined by three other Newcastle musicians whom they had known for a while. Their claim to the old group name had never been in doubt, as the two joint lead vocalists had always been the public face of the group anyway, and the powers-that-be at Charisma made it clear they favoured the continuity of keeping the old handle of what was easily their best-selling act. As Jacka said: 'The first band built up a good reputation and it would have been rather a waste to throw that all away'.[2] Guitarist Charlie Harcourt had been playing in America in Cat Mother and the All-Night Newsboys, but he had known them since they were teenagers, going 'way back to singing Buddy Holly songs with Hully outside a local West End of Newcastle fish and chip shop'.[3] New bass guitarist Tommy Duffy had been a member of Gary Wright's Wonderwheel, while drummer Paul Nichols came from Kenny's other previous group The Elcort.

In April 1973, Billy Mitchell was formally invited by Ray, Rod, and Si to join their new group. They had toyed with the idea of calling themselves The Corvettes, but then rejected it on the grounds that it sounded like a rock 'n' roll revival outfit. Instead, they chose a name from a phrase Rick Parfitt of Status Quo had used while they were touring Australia—Jack the Lad. Later that month, they began recording in Island Studios and, from the sessions, 'One More Dance' (a song by Rod) was issued as a single in May.

At around the same time, Charisma threw a Silver and Gold party at which the new Lindisfarne and the Jack the Lad line-ups were formally presented. They were also awarded a gold disc for sales of *Fog on the Tyne* and silver discs for *Nicely out Of Tune* and *Dingly Dell*. Such figures would never be equalled by subsequent album releases. *Pipedream* was issued in July and entered the charts at No. 29, only to disappear after two further weeks. It would, however, be the only Lindisfarne offshoot release, on album or single for that matter, ever to make the British chart.

To their irritation, almost immediately afterwards, Charisma released *Lindisfarne Live*, a recording of part of the 1971 Newcastle concert. It had only been intended as a BBC programme soundtrack, with considerable doctoring on the tapes in the studio afterwards. According to Roy Thomas Baker, who was credited as co-producer with Mickey Sweeney, it had been made by plugging into the back of their PA mixing desk. They took it back to Trident where he listened to it, and the result was so terrible that they had to add a few overdubs:

> We even overdubbed the audience, if you can understand that—we had to get people in the studio pretending that they were the audience and singing along, because there were no audience tracks for the singalong songs they did.[4]

Released in a mid-price range at the same time as a live Genesis album, it spent six weeks in the chart, reaching a high of No. 25. The group were annoyed about not having been consulted over the release of what they considered a sub-standard product; Alan was also sure that it would detract from the sales of *Pipedream.*

By this time, however, he was fired up by the birth of the new group, particularly with the new input from having more writers in the line-up. Previously, on record he had written 90 per cent of the material and they stood or fell on those songs. 'That's not to decry the old group,' he said, 'because it was good and it reached some fine creative peaks, but we just couldn't go any further musically. We couldn't satisfy ourselves.'[5] Lindisfarne Mk II, he believed, had 'better musicianship, new songs, and a slightly more professional approach'. In the future, he hoped they would be able to phase out the old material from their live set: 'I don't mind playing it. It's just lost its brilliance to me. I just sort of do it automatically'.[6]

In September, they returned to Trident Studios to record a fourth album, under the working title of *Don't Rip It ... I'll Take It By The Yard.* When it came to selecting tracks for inclusion for what saw the light of day as *Roll On, Ruby,* only four of Alan's songs were used, alongside three from Tommy, including 'Goodbye' (an uncertain-sounding closing song that gave the impression that none of the line-up were quite sure they would ever be able to repeat the experiment) and another three co-written by Charlie and Colin Gibson. Of Alan's numbers, 'When the War is Over' was hailed as classic Hull, notwithstanding the world-weary lyric, while the riff-driven 'Steppenwolf', with its punchy lead guitar and electric piano leading to a crescendo with strings and brass, served notice of a new group that rocked far harder than the old one ever did on record. The opening track, 'Taking Care of Business', was a damning indictment of the music industry and a warning about how musicians should all have degrees in business so they would realise if or when their managers were ripping them off. Alan's lyric told the tale of writing a song, hearing it on Radio 1, and then being told by the manager that he has already spent the money going up and down the country—after which he insists, 'You know how I'm fair, you can sign to the company for another ten years.'

Max Middleton, formerly keyboard player with The Jeff Beck Group, provided orchestral arrangements, while Roy Thomas Baker, who had known Kenny Craddock when he was a member of Ginger Baker's Airforce and who had been involved with *Pipedream* as engineer, as well as co-producing the live album, returned as producer. For him it was a strange combination:

I don't think it ever actually worked, because it was a combination of my—for want of a better word—over-production techniques, and their desire to cut as many corners as they could, to make it seem as though they were raw and down to earth. We tried to make it happen, but it still didn't quite work.[7]

Alan was much more blunt. He later said that Roy had been brought in to 'try to keep the squabbling factions at bay while he got on with the job', that *Roll On, Ruby* was 'a horrible album to make', and that it had been produced by committee or, as the sleeve credit would have it, 'by Roy T. Baker in conjunction with Mickey Sweeney and Lindisfarne'.[8] Though Jacka was less critical of the record, he admitted that it was something of a rushed job: 'We crammed it in between one lot of gigs and another. We're quite pleased with the final result—the only problem is we know it could have been better'.[9]

The front of the sleeve included a painting of a tree in leaf with a small, undeveloped branch sawn off and falling to the ground, while along the trunk, in discreet tiny lettering (evidently to avoid a high street record shop ban), were the words 'Fuck Off'. Ray thought the 'not-so-hidden' message was probably directed at Jack the Lad, but it never bothered him. He had after all played on *Pipedream* within a couple of months of the split earlier that year, and he knew all the new members of the new line-up well: 'I think the idea probably came from the sleeve designer and the group went along with it. Bit of a non-event really'.[10]

The new rocking outfit were 'a different type of band to the first line-up that had been so popular,' according to Kenny Craddock: 'We certainly didn't even try to achieve that distinctive "Lindisfarne sound" that the original band had'.[11] Their stage shows bore this out as they continued to play 'Lady Eleanor', 'We Can Swing Together', and 'No Time to Lose', alongside songs from *Pipedream* and the new album. Reviewers noticed they were no longer the amplified folk outfit they had seemed to be at the height of their success. The ever-supportive Jerry Gilbert in *Sounds* praised the new repertoire, 'a dichotomy with the exceptional songs of Hull on one side, and the crisp hoedown guitar duet of Craddock and Harcourt on the other'.[12] With the powerful playing of both, he said, plus Tommy's admittedly sometimes overpowering bass, this was a much louder six-piece group.

Some reviewers were happy to welcome the change, but Alan felt that while they were great company to be with, 'it just wasn't happening on stage'. Audiences were positive and gigs were sold out, yet some journalists evidently found what they were seeing and hearing a little too much of a culture shock. He said that 'it got my goat' when they had a new repertoire of songs they had been working on, and people just kept on asking for songs from the previous albums. He was neither the first nor the last rock star to learn that so often fans would prefer the old material.

Kenny agreed that the two Lindisfarne Mk II albums were much harder and more rock 'n' roll orientated. For him, it was not so much a case of Alan and Jacka particularly wanting to distance themselves from the old sound, more a matter of their seeking a change of direction. With the chemistry of new musicians in the line-up, that was the way it happened:

> Some of the things we tried didn't really work out and normally those things would have been ironed out in rehearsal or dropped before we went out on the road, or whatever; the trouble was that we were in a position where Lindisfarne already had a tour lined up, with people booking tickets for to see them, so we just went straight out with what we already had.

He thought the audience reaction was very good at the gigs, which were all packed out, but 'in the music press it was abysmal, they tore the arse out it'.[13] They were still playing the hits from the original line-up (excluding 'Meet Me on the Corner', being one of Rod's songs) and omitting some old numbers that they felt simply would not have worked with the new group. Much of the setlist comprised songs from the new album, and towards the end of the tour, they introduced some of Alan's older material, while reworking it to suit their style.

It worked best of all in America, where they could play without the audience having any preconception of how Lindisfarne should sound, so they could perform exactly how they wanted and without critics wondering what had happened to the group they knew and loved:

> We toured the States for about six weeks and to say that we really took off there would be a bit of a sweeping statement, but we had some great nights and got to play with some good bands, on the same bill with people like Little Feat and Traffic. All of the Geordie stuff went by the board of course, they just didn't understand it, but by the end of the tour Alan had written some new material for the next album and the band were pretty tight—you had to be, playing support to the likes of Little Feat. It raises your sights just a bit![14]

Although they went down well in America, their reception was not mirrored in record sales on either side of the Atlantic. Alan was more disillusioned than the others by poor sales of the album when it failed to chart in Britain. It was a major blow for a group that had topped the listings with one and enjoyed Top 10 success with the other two only a year earlier. They appeared on *The Old Grey Whistle Test* in March 1974 performing 'Taking Care of Business', which came out as a single at the same time and was chosen by Noel Edmonds as his Record of the Week on the Radio 1 breakfast show—ironically, perhaps, in view of the lyric and its satirical inclusion of the name of the station. However, the song did nothing to reverse their fading fortunes. An appearance at Charlton Athletic Football Club, headlined by The Who, with Bad Company and Humble Pie also on the bill, was enthusiastically received, but it failed to bring them any long-term benefits.

Jack the Lad was by all accounts a much happier experience on the whole for those involved. Ray said they had some great new songs, and he really enjoyed the opportunity to start again and put all the bad band politics behind him. There was some rivalry between Jack the Lad and Lindisfarne, with Alan dismissively calling his former colleagues' outfit a 'skiffle group' on occasion. Yet Ray and Billy always had a good relationship with all the new group, and they often met up for a drink or turned up at each others' gigs. 'For the first year or so Rod and Si were a little more reserved when it came to inter-band socialising which is fair enough,' said Ray, 'Si had been seen as dispensable and Rod got both barrels from Alan via the lyrics of 'Blue Murder''. However, he opined that both groups 'made some great music, had a lot of fun and made many friends around the world'.[15] As he continued to play on Alan's solo albums, by and large everything had turned out satisfactorily.

Behind 'Blue Murder', one of the songs on *Pipedream*, lay an interesting saga. In effect, it was Alan's equivalent of John Lennon's diatribe against Paul McCartney, 'How Do You Sleep'. Rod believed it was an open secret that the lyrics were all about him:

I used to wear makeup occasionally (well, it was the '70s! Not so much glam, more Keith Richards (fail)). I think the title refers to my blues influences and my desire to retain them as an element of the band's music, which was maybe contrary to what Alan wanted to do at the time, despite the fact that his rockier songs obviously contain blues elements, and the rest of us (the former Downtown Faction) were well able and keen to enhance that. I think Alan held me partially responsible for the band's 1973 split, which was definitely not the case—that arose from Alan being pretty unbearable and hardly speaking to the rest of us for about a year, then announcing that he wanted to replace Si (which I resisted), then announcing to the press that the band was splitting before it had been fully discussed or agreed between us. In the last verse, 'you're gonna have to learn to push', I take as a reference to the fact that I'm not a very pushy or competitive person, which Alan felt you had to be to 'get on in the music business'. I've no idea what my 'nice new brush' was. Despite all that, I loved Alan (though he could be infuriating), we had our own personal naughty shared humour, and we had some fun escapades together.[16]

Rod retaliated some years later, but much more subtly, with 'Dead Man's Karaoke', a song on one of his solo albums. By then, Alan was no longer around to hear it.[17]

Billy was a much less prolific writer than Alan, and the first album, *It's...Jack the Lad*, showed a fairer balance of compositions from Rod and Si. Recorded at Olympic Studios in Barnes in November and December 1973, it was produced by Hugh Murphy, who had overseen Alan's first solo single. Billy contributed five numbers, while Rod had three and Si two. Among Rod's was 'Why Can't I be Satisfied', a song that had lain on the shelf since being recorded and then rejected during the *Fog on the Tyne* sessions. Released as a single at around this time, it vied with 'Meet Me on the Corner' as one of his most infectious tunes ever. One of Si's numbers, 'Rosalee', was almost a 1920s pastiche, while the other, 'Song Without a Band', featured a guest vocal from Maddy Prior of Steeleye Span. Traditional folk returned to the fold with an eight-minute medley of jigs and reels. As Rod said, it was good for them to be able to use 'all these ideas that had been lying about that couldn't get used in Lindisfarne'. Billy was easy to get along with, and the genuine good vibe to their sessions was reflected in the music. Although never recorded, in the early days, their live show also included The Beatles' 'I Saw Her Standing There'. Nevertheless, a comparison between their debut album and *Roll On, Ruby* made it obvious which group had adhered more to their folk-based roots and which one had not.

It was perhaps a little ironic in the light of Rod's insistence the previous year that they were moving more into rock music. He had recently been going back to albums by Fairport Convention, and extending his own interest in the fiddle, a mood that he expanded on with a renewed passion:

> You can get a tremendous feel going because there's room for improvisation but those traditional things have an emotional and mythological interest that the blues doesn't have. I want to get back to the kind of things we liked around the time of *Liege and Lief*—a sort of Beatles/Fairport synthesis as well as our songs translated through that ethos.[18]

Moreover, they now relished the additional freedom they had in not being dominated by one very prolific writer:

I think that's something we fell down on, playing Alan's songs all the time; he doesn't always write that kind of song and I suppose, to an extent, we were beginning to feel like sidemen as a result. So in the end it became stifled—not through any fault of Alan's at all.[19]

Rod only remained with Jack the Lad for one album, and left shortly after it was released. He believed they were 'not getting anywhere', and decided that, for the time being, he had had enough of being in a group, being 'a bit envious of the looser way of doing things which had taken hold in the States' in contrast to the more rigid British approach.[20] Ray and Billy initially invited Rab Noakes to come and take his place, and when he said no, they recruited two members of fellow Geordie group Hedgehog Pie, bass guitarist Phil Murray and multi-instrumentalist Ian 'Walter' Fairbairn on guitar, mandolin, fiddle, and banjo. After both had come to see Rod's final gig at Liverpool Stadium, the new five-piece group went to rehearse and record a second album.

With one of their star songwriters gone, the group moved further into traditional folk, drawing on a rich seam of north-eastern music. Of the eleven tracks on *The Old Straight Track*, another Hugh Murphy production and released in September 1974, five were old traditional songs and instrumentals. 'Oakey Strike Evictions' was a number taken from the repertoire of Tommy Armstrong, the late nineteenth-century 'Bard of the Northern Coalfield'. As for originals, Si came into his own as the sole writer of four songs and Billy contributed one. If the album was not a success in terms of sales, it received stellar reviews and became *Melody Maker*'s Folk Album of the Year. It was followed a few weeks later by a non-album single, Rod's final group contribution, the jaunty 'Home Sweet Home'.

According to Billy, *The Old Straight Track* was a venture into the unknown. Si said that when they recorded it, the group were still feeling their way and it 'certainly went in a strange direction':

> [But recording it] was the 'funnest' time of my musical life. We were pushing the boundaries of our progressive-folk roots and taking Fairport/Steeleye type liberties with the arrangements.[21]

It came as a surprise to Hugh, who had probably been expecting them to come up with something similar to the first album—'how wrong can you be'.

Yet Charisma were still hellbent on that elusive hit for Jack the Lad, and according to Billy, they hated the second album because there was no obvious single on it. Two or three years earlier, it had been possible to establish groups as album sellers without a hit 45 first, *Fog on the Tyne* being a prime example. However, by 1974, 7-inch vinyls—to capture the ear of Radio 1 daytime presenters and producers, and accordingly sell well—were increasingly established as the norm.

Whereas the first line-up of Jack the Lad had taken itself fairly seriously—with Billy realising that to some extent he was seen as being in competition with Alan—the second line-up became well-known for letting its hair down and having fun on stage. Some audiences had memories of the group, or some of them, dancing around like lunatics on stage and having everyone in stitches, or performing a 'mime' sequence that involved sculpting an Adam and Eve statue, complete with necessary appendages. It all loses something in cold print, but a hilarious time was had by all, yet never at the expense of quality musicianship.

On a more serious note, at one of their gigs at South Bank Polytechnic on 5 October 1974, five people were killed and sixty-five injured when a couple of bombs were detonated by the Irish Republican Army at two pubs in Guildford. Among those accused of involvement and subsequently arrested was seventeen-year-old Carole Richardson, who had been in the audience at the show and had a photograph of herself to prove it. Despite her alibi and the group's supporting evidence of her innocence, she was imprisoned for conspiracy and not released until 1989.

Billy was mildly annoyed when the press kept on comparing Jack the Lad and Lindisfarne. One music paper printed reviews of *The Old Straight Track* and *Happy Daze* in the same column. 'As it happened, ours came out better,' he said, 'but it wasn't a nice thing to do.'[22]

Roll On, Ruby was Lindisfarne's last album for Charisma. 'Fog on the Tyne' was belatedly issued as a single in July 1974 without promotion or expectation, just as their new manager Tony Dimitriades was obtaining them a new deal with Warner Brothers. An eighteen-track compilation album, *Lindisfarne's Finest Hour*, came out in the autumn of 1975 and crept into the Top 60 for one week. It contained all previously released material, apart from the apparently accidental inclusion of the alternate version of 'Meet Me on the Corner'.

Yet it was too late for a fresh start, as an increasingly disillusioned Alan led them into the studio at the house of Trevor Morais, drummer with The Peddlers, for what was to be a 'make-or-break' album. Of his five songs that comprised *Happy Daze*, released in September 1974 and produced by Eddie Offord, at least three—'You Put the Laff on Me', 'No Need to Tell Me', and 'Gin and Tonix All Round'—suggested an abiding bitterness, perhaps directed at former colleagues or management, or maybe even both. A painting on the back of the sleeve, showing two chimpanzees sitting on a desert island weighing bags of money and surrounded by sharks with percentage signs on their fins, did nothing to convey an impression of 'happy days'.

Kenny and Tommy each contributed three songs, with Tommy's 'Tonight' being chosen as the single. Powered by an infectious guitar riff, it was undoubtedly potential chart fare, but radio interest was not forthcoming. Kenny Craddock was pleased with the experience of *Happy Daze*, believing that working with Eddie Offord, who had also been involved in the production of Yes's albums, had made a difference for the better:

> Everyone was putting songs forward, including one or two that I had, and a lot of the songs on that album were recorded outside, which was great. Songs like 'River', you know, with two of us playing acoustic guitar, Jacka playing mandolin and the sounds of birds and the little babbling brook were just recorded live—it all added to the 'ambience' of the recording.[23]

Jacka likewise found the new Lindisfarne an enjoyable venture in musical terms. Now they had two new writers in Kenny and Tommy, they were enjoying the more rocky, adventurous musical approach. He had moreover been inspired to begin writing songs himself with Charlie, the former concentrating on lyrical content while the latter 'hoyed' the chords around. Unfortunately for them, the group did not stay together long enough for any of their collaborations to be recorded or performed just yet.

Sadly for both of them at least, in Britain, reviews for the record were mostly poor, not to say savage. One music paper called it 'a dismal experience', though another praised Eddie Offord for his work on the album and his 'excellent job of the production which [was] really crisp, buoyant and colourful, with horns augmenting the group here and there'.[24] Minimal sales for the album and lack of radio interest in the single suggested that all but the most devoted fans, in Britain at least, had lost interest.

By now, Alan had had enough of touring, and felt that the group had completely lost direction. Within six months of the first album, he had felt that 'it just wasn't going to work, so [he] just got on with it and got out as soon as [he] could'. The material they recorded as Lindisfarne Mk II did not deserve the name, he maintained, and the group 'should have been strangled at birth'.[25] Combined sales of both their albums had amounted to less than those of *Pipedream* of its own.

The others were keen to carry on, especially Jacka and Tommy, who felt that their third album would undoubtedly be their definitive one—but there was no third album. In February 1975, during another British tour, it was announced that it would be their last. For Alan, Lindisfarne had gone as far as they possibly could 'within the existing format of the band', and after honouring their remaining live commitments, they would disband. He was planning to record and release a second solo album, while Jacka, Charlie, and Tommy intended to continue together under another name. The last date of the tour was to be at the Odeon, Newcastle, at the end of February—at which Ray Laidlaw and Yes drummer Alan White both made a surprise appearance onstage during the encore—but demand for additional tickets resulted in a few extra gigs in March.

An interview with Alan shortly after the news broke found him in a bitter, if unapologetic frame of mind. He had spent all his life writing songs, he said, and he thought they deserved a more considered opinion: 'I think I'm one of the best songwriters ever to come out of Britain. I know it sounds egotistical, but I think it's about time I was taken more seriously'.[26]

The split also had a sour side for Jacka, though for a different reason. Once the group was no more, Alan took all the equipment except for Jacka's mandolin and harmonicas. Debts had accrued and Jacka was served a writ for unpaid VAT, which he had wrongly assumed was being taken care of by their then management company. With a wife and two small children to support, and no songwriting royalties coming in, he had to take on a window cleaning round and decorating jobs on Tyneside.

Like four of the other five, he had been shocked and disappointed when Alan pulled the plug. Even if the line-up of musicians on *Pipedream* had been Alan's first choice, the five supporting members who went on to comprise Lindisfarne Mk II had put a great deal of time and effort into the group, and they were all finding and developing their own style right up to the end. Perhaps it was not what Alan had in mind, Jacka suggested later:

> He never said anything to the contrary at the time. The Americans liked us, as most hadn't heard the original band and had no preconceived idea of what had gone before. We weren't judged or compared with the old band, as was the case in Britain and Europe. We did some storming shows and I still think we might have made it over there if we had stayed together.[27]

Billboard called *Happy Daze* the best album that had yet been released under the name of Lindisfarne, but such praise came too late. Kenny and Tommy agreed it was a shame when they broke up, but in retrospect maybe it was the right time. A third album would have been the definitive one, 'but it had all become a committee thing'.[28] However, the impression remained that a dissatisfied Alan had decided to draw down the curtain on them without agreement and minimal, if any, consultation with the rest of them.

Ironically, it would be Rod Clements who benefited most from chart success at this time, even if his name was not on the record label. During the autumn of 1974, Jack the Lad had toured to packed houses as the opening act for Ralph McTell. He had just re-recorded 'Streets of London', a song of his that had previously appeared on an album five years earlier and had since become a contemporary folk standard. When he invited Rod to play bass guitar on it, he asked him to make a point of playing it in the same style of the opening section of 'Meet Me on the Corner' as he thought the latter sounded rather like 'Streets' speeded up. Also, including Prelude on backing vocals, the result became the title track of Ralph's next album and a single that radio stations and record buyers took to heart at once—it was a No. 2 hit in January 1975.

The object of the exercise had really been to provide a Christmas hit single for Bert Jansch—and for Charisma—with a new version of 'In the Bleak Midwinter'. Now something of a veteran of the British folk scene, both as a soloist and as member of Pentangle, Bert was still something of a cult figure whose commercial success outside the group had always been negligible. In September, he had released a solo album on the label, *L.A. Turnaround*, produced by and featuring former Monkees guitarist Michael Nesmith, and the label was keen to promote him with a hit in some form. 'In the Bleak Midwinter' was recorded first, with Rod on bass and Ralph as producer. After it was completed, journalist Pete Frame, who was present at the session, uncorked a bottle of Chambertin to toast the record's future success. As they still had some spare time left in the studio, Ralph suggested more or less on the spur of the moment that they should join him on a new version of 'Streets'. Both singles were released at the same time, but 'Midwinter' was the one that was met with indifference and failed to chart.

Rod was enjoying the freedom of being a freelance bass player, and also worked with Michael Chapman at around this time, in spite of Michael having been told by Rick Kemp (bass guitarist of Steeleye Span and a mutual friend) that he had been a member of Lindisfarne. He had seen the group two or three years earlier at the Bilzen Festival in Belgium, performing one night while somewhat the worse for drink, and he thought they were terrible. Fortunately, he did not hold the experience against Rod, and both benefited from the collaboration, which resulted in Rod playing on a couple of his albums.

Another meeting that might have borne fruit, but never came to anything, occurred when Mark Knopfler suddenly turned up on Rod's doorstep at Finchley with his guitar. Mark had been a member of Brewers Droop and was playing with various other musicians just for fun while considering his next move, and holding down a job as a lecturer in English at Loughton College, Essex. Both of them started jamming and recorded an instrumental by Mark for two acoustic guitars, 'Newport Mount Rag'. Mark then invited him to join the group that he was thinking of forming, but Rod declined as he had had enough of being in groups for the time being, although they remained in touch. Mark also became a friend of Si, and he used to bring his group round to Si's kitchen to rehearse in their early days. Legend has it that this was where they eventually hit on a perfect name for what would be one of the most successful British groups of the next decade—Dire Straits.

Shortly before Lindisfarne Mk II reached the end of the road, Alan had been pursuing a new direction. In the autumn of 1974, he was asked to write the soundtrack for and star in *Squire*, a television play written by Tom Pickard, part of the BBC2 series *Second City Firsts*. His role was that of jobless Alfy, who enters a fantasy world as a member of the idle rich, struggles to come to terms with mental and marital breakdown, and at the end throws himself into the Tyne. The solo album that Warner Bros had asked Alan to write, record, and produce as part of the contract signed before *Happy Daze* was made was to be called *Captain Benwell* after the part of Newcastle in which he was born, but then became *Squire*. Part of the reason was financial, as Alan was responsible for large debts left by Lindisfarne after the split and the other members had very little money. *Squire* was therefore recorded quickly on a tight budget, with several of the musicians from *Pipedream*, including Jacka and Kenny, Ray on the few days when he was not working with Jack the Lad, Colin Gibson on bass guitar, plus Albert Lee and future Whitesnake guitarist Micky Moody on one track each. One song, 'Dan the Plan', was about T. Dan Smith, a former Newcastle City Council leader who served a prison sentence for corruption.

Derek Taylor, the former Beatles' press officer, was Vice-President of Marketing at Warner Bros at the time. During a break in the recording sessions for *Squire*, Alan, Tony Dimitriades, and others were having a meal with some of the staff when the place suddenly went quiet. George Harrison, who had arrived on business as he was working with others at Warner Bros in connection with his label, Dark Horse, walked in and came to sit next to Alan, greeting him with a cheery 'hello, squire'. Both talked about songwriting, and then they all returned to the office where Derek proceeded to play some of the completed album. George told Alan that he sounded a 'bit like John', to which Alan promptly informed the former Beatle that there was a song on the other where he sounded 'a bit like [George]!'[29]

After the album was completed, receiving good reviews but again poor sales and no chart success, Derek suggested that Alan should write and record a really commercial single. The result was *Crazy Woman*, but it went the same way as the others. His records with the label had come nowhere near recouping the advances, *Happy Daze* having sold only about 1,500 copies, and Derek Taylor had to drop him from the label, but not without a very friendly, apologetic letter wishing him well. With Glen Colson now managing him, Alan did a few solo dates in various venues around the country, some with Tom Robinson's Café Society as support, but audiences were small, albeit appreciative.

Glen then suggested that they should try and form a British equivalent of Crosby, Stills and Nash. Alan and Rab Noakes were to have been two-thirds of the unit, with either Nick Lowe, from the recently disbanded Brinsley Schwarz, or Gerry Rafferty, whose group Stealers Wheel had become a duo with Joe Egan for recording purposes only and then acrimoniously split. Glen then stated that it was dream to form a supergroup, particularly as Alan could hardly do it by himself if he was only drawing crowds of a hundred or so, but nothing came of it.

Alan then returned home to Tyneside to ponder his next move. About a year later, he found his songwriting muse again and went into the studios to record demos of six numbers that were the result of ten days' work, including 'I Wish You Well' and 'Easy and Free'. Barbara Hayes set up a meeting with Abe Hock, a native of Los Angeles who had worked in record promotion and helped to set up Led Zeppelin's Swan Song label. On the strength of Alan's demos, he agreed to become his new manager and promptly secured him a deal with Rocket Records, the label established by Elton John, who had been a long-time admirer of Alan and his work.

For Jack the Lad, it was approaching make or break time. They were as welcome at the BBC as Lindisfarne had once been, recording eight sessions for John Peel between May 1973 and September 1976, plus one for Bob Harris and a show in the Radio 1 series *Sounds on Sunday*. John was a fervent champion of their music from the start, writing appreciatively in his *Sounds* column of one of his roadshows in February 1975 at Tiffany's, Newcastle. They played alongside Medicine Head, Snafu, and Jack the Lad, who had played 'a crisp little set (sounds like a lettuce, doesn't it?) crammed with amusing songs, jigs and reels to set the feet a dancin', dancin' all your cares away, and an atmosphere of Geordified rowdiness'.[30]

That summer the group released a third album, recorded at Sound Techniques, Chelsea, and produced by Simon Nicol, who was at that time on a four-year sabbatical from Fairport Convention. Billy and Si each contributed four songs, with three traditional numbers also included. One of the latter was 'Gentleman Soldier', which for the intro used the four-part harmony section from 'Twist and Shout' and had a break featuring John Kirkpatrick on accordion. Released as a single, it attracted some airplay—

especially from John Peel, who called it 'one of the most joyous records [he had] ever heard in [his] life' and placed it at No. 3 in his favourite singles of the year in his Radio 1 show shortly before Christmas. In a year that would later see Steeleye Span's 'All Around My Hat' and Mike Oldfield's 'In Dulci Jubilo' both become Top 5 singles, 'Gentleman Soldier' would not have been out of place in the charts, but it still failed to sell. A similar fate awaited the album's second single, Billy's 'Rocking Chair'. The song featured an appearance by Jacka on harmonica and he also contributed an engaging design for the album sleeve.

Although the group found Simon 'a bit of a slave driver' in the studio, the album proved an agreeable experience to record. Producer and musicians got on very well together, and Simon found them 'such nice, outgoing chaps,' even though it was an expensive business keeping Walter well supplied with Carlsberg Special at 10.30 a.m.

It was followed by what was arguably the height of their broadcasting career, an appearance on BBC2's *The Old Grey Whistle Test*, at that time the polar opposite of *Top of the Pops* in concentrating on album-orientated acts. Presented by Bob Harris between 1972 and 1978, it was sometimes seen as a little over-earnest and reverential—until Jack the Lad appeared on 28 October 1975. They closed the show with 'Rocking Chair' and 'Gentleman Soldier', followed by (in Billy's words) 'a bit of Geordie culture'—a demonstration of the Morris dance, complete with shovels and miner's lamps. The routine had long been a much-loved part of their stage show, but to television viewers to whom 'dance' meant the slickly choreographed routines of Pan's People on *Top of the Pops*, it was probably nothing short of a revelation.

Yet endorsements from music press, Bob Harris on *Whistle Test* and from John Peel on his late night Radio 1 show were not exactly sending records flying out of the shops. After *Rough Diamonds*, Billy thought, there was a distinct cooling towards the group from the young guns at Charisma, who were their management and agency as well as record company:

> We weren't playing the kind of stuff that they were into, there was a change in the air, the London pub band circuit seemed to be the thing with bands like Bees Make Honey, and The Kursaal Flyers, becoming flavour of the month.[31]

The label could console itself with the fact that their investment with Genesis was beginning to pay off, and they were at last turning into the major album sellers that Lindisfarne had once been. It had enjoyed some success with five Monty Python albums and attracted considerable publicity with two albums on which Sir John Betjeman, the Poet Laureate, recited some of his work set to music. However, apart from one Top 10 single each by Clifford T. Ward and Gary Shearston, its overall performance over the previous couple of years had been patchy. It had seen its most successful signing fragment into acts who could make neither the singles nor album charts, and between them yield one solo album that had just nudged the Top 30. Many a fan, as well as those within the company—and probably members of the groups themselves—must have realised that a Billy Mitchell-fronted Lindisfarne, continuing to record Alan Hull's material and play it onstage while he took a less visible role, and come up with radio-friendly singles to continue to generate interest in subsequent albums, would have been the better business option.

Barbara Hayes, who had remained Jack the Lad's publisher, accordingly sought them a new recording deal as well as management and agency, and came up with all three at United Artists. After rehearsals in Devon, they went to Wessex Sound Studios, Highbury, in the summer of 1976 to record with producer Tom Allom. With their new deal, they were under pressure to get a fourth album down.

The rehearsals were plagued by domestic issues. Si's marriage was in trouble, his wife had been seeing the group's roadie behind his back, and the rest of the group were distracted by the unhappy couple's persistent late-night rows. With reluctance, they had to ask Si to resolve the matter amicably or consider his position. The sessions had become very 'stop/start' and he was not really contributing, so everything was put on hold and they went home for a while. As recording time had been booked, they had to go ahead without him. It was a difficult time for them all, said Billy:

> …hearts ruling heads on one side, and vice versa. I was the biggest culprit in pushing for 'business as usual', which caused Si to leave the band, a regrettable decision for all, as JTL was never the same again. Lucky for me, Si never held a grudge, and we have remained firm friends.[32]

Si was not replaced and one of his songs, 'See How They Run', had been recorded as a demo, but it was not proceeded with any further for the time being. The group was accordingly augmented in the studio by a horn section, Jacka on harmonica and Andy Bown from Status Quo on keyboards, while Billy ended up writing six of the ten songs on the album. There were two traditional tunes, but most of it saw them moving in a more pop-rock direction. The two singles, 'Eight Ton Crazy', written by Andy Fairweather Low, and Billy's 'Trinidad', with steel drums described approvingly by some as 'a Geordie reggae song', were once again engaging, quality songs that in a kinder world would have been hits; however, airplay and sales still proved elusive.

The *Jackpot* album sleeve had already been designed. As it would have been too expensive to start all over again, in place of Si's photo on the front, they substituted a pic of the back of John Blackburn's head (their roadie). Billy stated that it was 'just after he had a perm (which made his head look like a blackberry). The things you do for love....'[33]

Jacka was invited to join the group on a full-time basis, but although he enjoyed the experience of playing with them, he found their style of music a little removed from the direction he was taking. Keen to pursue a solo career, he had hoped to record further with Warner Bros, but they were uninterested in retaining him, particularly after the failure of *Happy Daze*. Apart from playing on Chris de Burgh's first album (*Far Beyond These Castle Walls*) in 1975, he was finding session work hard to come by.

That same year, Barry McKay, who would soon play an important managerial role in Lindisfarne's affairs, negotiated a publishing deal for him and the songs he was writing with Charlie Harcourt, and a solo contract with EMI whereby three solo singles would be released within a year, plus the option of an album. An advance was secured, but it was quickly used up in the efforts to get a band on the road. Captain Whizzo consisted of Jacka and Charlie, plus guitarist Robert Barton (who had released a solo single the previous year, 'Benwell Lad', featuring Jacka and Alan Hull), bass guitarist Jimmy Wylie, and drummer Colin Mason. They only played three dates together before disbanding, Jacka conceding ruefully that he had 'got the wrong people'. Producer Muff Winwood heard the demos of his songs, and was sufficiently impressed with them to give Jacka the confidence he needed to go into the studio as a solo artist. Two of the songs he and Charlie had co-written, 'Take Some Time' and 'Working On', were recorded in June and released as a single two months later. It sank without trace, and that was the end of Jacka's career as a soloist for the time being, although EMI had not heard the last of their involvement.

Barry proved an asset as a manager, and was determined to try and maintain a career in the music business for his eager client. Now free of The Faces, who had disbanded a year earlier, Rod Stewart was about to go on tour. Barry approached his management with a view to Ray joining him for live dates, especially as the singer was keen to play 'Maggie May' and 'Mandolin Wind' and reproduce the recorded versions as faithfully as possible on stage. However, he required a musician who could also play guitar and piano, so the idea never went any further. Fortunately, other doors soon opened. After Jacka and Charlie had played some folk clubs as a duo, they formed Harcourt's Heroes, with Colin Mason from Captain

Whizzo, plus saxophonist Marty Craggs and bass guitarist Barry Spence. By playing local pubs and clubs, with a couple of residencies at Whitley Bay and Heaton that were regularly packed out, and not rushing into the big time, Jacka reckoned that they were now earning at least as much, if not more than he ever did with Lindisfarne Mk II. At the same time, he was commissioned by producer Malcolm Gerrie to write theme music for various Tyne Tees television programmes. He found it a challenge and not very interesting—but it was better than cleaning windows.

Everybody from the old group had kept their hand in, in some way or other. Rod was still happy as a freelance musician. After working with Michael Chapman and then Ralph McTell, he had joined Rab Noakes on tour in a group that also included Charlie Harcourt on guitar and Pick Withers (the drummer who had worked with Mark Knopfler in Brewers Droop and would shortly join him in Dire Straits). Further work with Bert Jansch followed, producing an album for him and playing as part of his group on a tour of Denmark and Sweden. After leaving Jack the Lad, Si joined them for a while, and then did a stint with the socialist 7:84 Theatre Group, which was looking for a guitarist and singer.

It was inevitable that sooner or later there would be demands for, or at the very least thoughts of, the original group getting back together again. Early in 1976, each former member was approached by Andy Hudson, Director of the Newcastle Festival, to ask if they would be prepared to reform for a one-off gig. The festival was held every autumn as a showcase for local music and culture, and what better attraction could there be than the city's most famous group? Each responded with varying degrees of interest. Jacka was the least enthusiastic of them all, acting partly on advice from Barry McKay who suggested caution. He advised that that if they did play together again, it would be such a major event on its own that it should not merely be just one of a series of events at the festival, but instead a standalone concert at Newcastle City Hall instead. The idea lingered, and from that came the suggestion that they ought to play there at Christmas.

From there, the idea continued to grow and grow as telephone conversations between the widely dispersed quintet ensued. Rod was abroad, Si in London, Ray on tour with Jack the Lad, Jacka working on and promoting his single, and Alan writing and recording another solo album. By early October, they had all agreed to do it as a one-off. In November, it was announced that they would play the City Hall on 22 and 23 December, but it would not be a permanent reunion. Even so, the news dominated Tyneside, and due to overwhelming demand, a third show was added on the second day. That also sold out in next to no time, and a fourth show was announced, with proceeds to be donated to the Newcastle *Evening Chronicle* Sunshine Fund and the Metro Radio Charity Appeal. At the same time, there was immediate interest from the BBC (which planned a documentary and a recording of the shows) and Metro Radio (which intended to record the shows). At this early stage, the group had yet to meet again in person.

At last they got together for the first time since that unhappy occasion in Tokyo at the end of that ill-fated tour in 1973, at Alan's home in Whickham. In time-honoured tradition, after an almost emotional hello, it was down to the local for appropriate refreshment. Over the next three days, they tried out songs in Alan's home studio, and on 21 December, held a full-scale rehearsal at the Pavilion Centre in nearby Westgate Road. Any initial unease had soon gone, and despite the separate musical projects with which they had all recently been involved, it was largely a matter of picking up from where they had left off.

At the concerts themselves, no detail had been spared to prepare audiences for a festive atmosphere. Everyone was offered a party hat on entry, Christmas carols were played on the City Hall organ by Russell Missin (principal organist and director of music at Newcastle Cathedral), and comedian Mike Elliott appeared as Santa Claus as he welcomed everyone from the stage as the curtain went up. The group's reception at the concerts was ecstatic, with everyone joining in enthusiastically on the old favourites. Si had his hair cut on stage and thrown to the audience. After the group had walked off to their dressing rooms backstage and the house lights went on, the audience continued to clap, stamp, and shout out for more, until they reappeared for a spontaneous five-part harmony version of 'White Christmas'.

Barry had arranged for a private party to take place at Scamps Discotheque immediately after the final show. Shortly before the last song that night, a visibly emotional Alan told the audience that there was going to be a party to celebrate afterwards—and everybody present was invited. A somewhat aghast Mr McKay immediately phoned the club to warn them that there might be a few extra guests. The management rose to the occasion, with the result that over 1,000 extra people turned up. Everybody was admitted, although it was almost impossible for anybody to move, but the group cheerfully chatted to fans and signed many autographs.

After the shows, they all went back to their respective projects. Jack the Lad realised they were coming to the end of the road, and with changes in the staff at United Artists, the label lost interest—any ideas anyone might have had of a fifth planned album went with it. They played their final gig at the Coatham Bowl, Redcar, in July 1977. Meanwhile, Si continued working with the 7:84 Theatre Group, while Rod returned to Scandinavia to play on a tour with Michael Chapman.

Alan's next solo album, and his first for Rocket Records, included Kenny Craddock, Pete Kirtley, Colin Gibson, and Ray Laidlaw playing on the sessions. Kenny, Peter, and Colin were gigging at the time with drummer Terry Popple under the name Radiator, and were keen to ask Alan to join as they wanted his songs and a front man. It was in a way a return to the situation with Brethren several years earlier. Radiator, which Alan saw as like a British version of Steely Dan, played several live gigs throughout 1977 and he found that working with them was giving him the buzz for playing live once more. One show at Newcastle City Hall featured Radiator as the headline act, with Harcourt's Heroes supporting.

As recording progressed, Alan was becoming increasingly enthusiastic about their material, and then, despite the advice of Rocket Records to the contrary, he decided that he would credit it to the group rather than release it as a solo album. There was a complication in that Kenny, Colin, Pete, and Terry were already gigging as Radiator, and Alan particularly wanted to use Ray, but was more or less committed to employing the whole group. They therefore decided to join forces and rehearse with two drummers. Ray loved the idea as much as the rest of them as he had already seen a few bands with two kits, including the early Mothers of Invention and Grateful Dead, and he felt that as long as he and his opposite number had a respect and understanding for each other's playing, as well as the music they were performing, then it could be a lot of fun:

> Terry and I decided who would be the rock on each track and who would do the flowering. We arranged a few parts to play in unison but most of it was done on the spur of the moment and it felt great.

Although they played several dates that year and enjoyed the experience, they were mostly in clubs, where it failed to prove cost-effective. In addition, it was the year of punk rock, where nearly anybody who had been around more than a few years was seen by some as lacking credibility: 'The new-wave bands were getting all the headlines so it was hard to progress and expensive to keep on the road'.[34] It may not have helped them that an Irish punk band, The Radiators from Space, had just completed a nationwide tour with Thin Lizzy to much acclaim. Having two outfits with such similar names was bound to result in confusion.

The Christmas concerts of 1976 had been such a success, and during the summer the group asked Barry if he could organise more of the same that year at the same venue. Ray suggested that, as they had never done a satisfactory live album, they ought to record the shows this time with a view to future release. Four dates scheduled for 21 to 24 December sold out quickly once again, and a fifth was arranged as a benefit for mentally and physically handicapped and underprivileged children.

At the same time, they were approached with offers to play a full British tour but declined. Inevitably, several labels made offers with contracts for new material, but they strongly denied that anything approaching a permanent reunion was on the cards. Jacka was probably the one most determined not to be part of a newly reformed Lindisfarne, stating that a reformation would be 'purely a nostalgia thing', which the Christmas concerts would be enough to satisfy. He had stuck it out for a long time with his own career, and was convinced that he would crack it next year. Yet the lure of the obvious would be impossible to resist.

5

'Run for Home'

The 1977 concerts at Newcastle took place with the same festive trimmings as before, including Russell Missin on the organ and Mike Elliott as Santa Claus. This time there were the added bonuses of the Killingworth sword dancers during 'We Can Swing Together', and a brass section on 'All Fall Down'. The final night's show, on Christmas Eve, was recorded by the Basing Street 24-track mobile studio. Ray acknowledged that by then they had a certain amount of distance, and were in a position to see where they had gone wrong last time. Neither Jack the Lad nor Lindisfarne Mk II had had the chemistry of the original group, a factor reinforced by record purchasing resistance—in other words, zero chart success all round. There were no hard feelings; on the contrary, the urge to start again and create music together as before was there. Despite his initial reluctance, Jacka now agreed with the general consensus, acknowledging that they had got everything out of their systems. When they got back together, he acknowledged, it was like they had never been away: 'We buried the hatchet on a lot of personal issues'.[1]

When pressed as to why they had gone their separate ways in the first place, Alan said he was not really clear why they did split up anyway. Yet he conceded that the magic had gone at the time and 'maybe [they] just needed a rest'. He never regretted the lost years: 'Now we're back together and it's working so well, it looks like it was a good idea. We needed that break. And we can handle it that much better this time'.[2]

In the first few weeks of 1978, the group went to Surrey Sound Studios to work on a few new songs. Barry McKay was now their official manager, and they had decided that any reunion would be dependent on the existence of quality new material. A month of rehearsals was lined up at Rockfield Studios, Monmouth. Gus Dudgeon, who had been Elton John's producer, had said he wanted to produce them ever since hearing 'Lady Eleanor'. Completed songs written by Alan, Si, and Jacka with Charlie were rehearsed and demoed.

One day, Alan was doodling on the piano while Ray looked through Alan's old school exercise book containing a list of all his song titles. There were some he was not familiar with, one being 'Run for Home'. He asked Alan to play it and he said, 'Oh that's not up to much, I wrote it after a really bad review for a solo gig when I was still living in London.' Ray nagged him to play it and after ten minutes or so he gave it a go. When he reached the first chorus, Jacka and Si joined in the singing:

> It sounded great. As it got to the second chorus Gus Dudgeon walked into the room, having just arrived. He listened as the lads completed the impromptu version of the song and then said, "Hello, I'm Gus, that's the first single."[3]

The song, which expressed Alan's yearning to go back to his own patch after having had his 'share of the breaks' and of 'the places in town where the faces hang round just to stare at each other', was recorded next day.

Ray found Gus 'meticulous about every aspect of recording', and he thought the tracks they cut with him as producer were the most sonically superior recordings they ever made. This was before the era of samplers and sequencers, and both of them—drummer and producer—spent a day and a half together getting the drum sound just right. Ray admitted that it had its down side:

> [I] glazed over after a few hours of comparing fifteen or twenty snare drums but when he [Gus] had finished switching mikes and moving stuff around the results were staggering. Again this is only my opinion but I think the recordings we made with Gus are the only real pop records in Lindisfarne's body of work. 'Run for Home' still sounds amazing to me.[4]

As ever, Si had a highly quotable take on the subject. He thought it took rather less time to get the guitar sound right—about five minutes, in fact: 'The recording engineer has a deal with the pub down the road. The musicians are going to end up down there on the first day anyway'.[5]

Back and Fourth, so named after Rod's suggestion because they were back and it was the fourth from the original line-up, was completed shortly before a new deal with Phonogram was signed. On 18 April, several weeks of speculation in the music weeklies ended as it was confirmed that Lindisfarne were back—and not just for Christmas.

For Alan and Ray, the only drawback was that it meant the end of Radiator. The other members were annoyed and felt they had been left in the lurch, said Ray, although Kenny and Terry forgave them: 'Don't know about the others [Colin and Pete]. I still feel bad about the way it finished, it was a great band'.[6]

The new record deal brought in its train another momentary problem, but with a straightforward solution. Alan had been incensed a few years earlier by a review in *Melody Maker*: '[It was not just] a slagging review of a solo concert that I thought was great', but a complete personal affront— 'There was no way it could be explained away'. When they signed with Phonogram, he found that the writer of the diatribe, Brian Harrigan, was now their press officer: 'The only thing I could think was that when I saw him, I was gonna kick his head in.... I didn't kick his head in. I got him to buy us a drink instead'. However, Alan had taken the attack in the paper to heart so much that he said he had 'stopped being part of the scene' for a while, had no manager, agent or record company for a while, stopped reading the music press and watching *Top of the Pops*, and left his home in Barnet to return to Newcastle. The situation had been largely responsible for the theme and lyrics of 'Run for Home'. It was a curious coincidence that Gerry Rafferty, the singer-songwriter with whom he had a certain amount in common (and with whom he might have teamed up in a group a couple of years previously) had also used his dissatisfaction with the music industry as inspiration for his return to the Top 10 at around the same time with the equally autobiographical 'Baker Street'. In both cases, the anger in the lyrics probably went over the heads of many who went out and bought the singles.

'Run for Home', backed with Si's 'Stick Together', was released as a single on the Mercury label at the end of April. It was warmly welcomed, received generous airplay on Radio 1 and 2, and saw the group on *Top of the Pops* for the first time in six years. They made four appearances on the show with the record on a slow but steady nine-week ascent of the charts as it reached a peak of No. 10, earning a silver disc for sales of 250,000 copies. Although not their highest-charting record, during its fifteen weeks in the Top 75, it became their best-selling British 45 ever.

The album was released in June. With nine songs by Alan and two from Jacka and Charlie, it was described by Ray as a deliberate attempt to make an American-sounding record—'a Geordie version of Fleetwood Mac'. The latter's unstoppable success with their previous album, *Rumours* (a record with across-the-board appeal), had been envied by every record company. On Lindisfarne's album, the closest to their old sound and the one that made the best use of Rod's fiddle was the most outspoken piece of social comment of all, Alan's 'Marshall Riley's Army'; it was about the Jarrow march of 1936, and the only track they had produced themselves. Despite any similarities to Fleetwood Mac and footsteps towards AOR territory, Alan was ready to allay suspicion that they were changing musical direction too much. 'There's no way we can ditch our folk influence,' he said, 'that's the way we are. There's no way you can ditch yourself.'[7]

A reviewer of the album in *Melody Maker* welcomed the group's return, while suggesting at the same time that Gus Dudgeon's strings had given them a gloss that moved them too close to the easy listening market and took off some of the Northern grit. The album peaked at No. 22 during an eleven-week stay on the charts, and was certified silver during the summer. Even more gratifying, perhaps, was the group's eagerly awaited (if only) breakthrough into the American Top 40 towards the end of the year, with the single reaching No. 33.

That summer, Lindisfarne were one of the headlining acts at the Reading Festival, taking pride of place on Saturday 24 August alongside Status Quo and The Motors. A couple of weeks later, another of Alan's songs from the album, 'Juke Box Gypsy', became the second single. Closer to the old Lindisfarne, with prominent mandolin and harmonica and a twanging, almost Duane Eddy-like lead guitar sound instead of strings, it received the *Top of the Pops* new release slot after a minor change to the lyrics, which were a touch risqué for the time: 'one more poke and she can do it all night' being swiftly altered to 'your magic medicine feels so fine'. However, it was not enough to help the record climb any further than its first week position of No. 56. A third single written by Alan, the non-album track 'Brand New Day', failed altogether.

Nevertheless, the group set off on a thirty-nine-date tour that autumn, with Chris Rea as support, to coincide with the release of *Magic in the Air*, the double live album featuring a recording of the Christmas Eve 1977 show. One of the first dates of the tour, at Essex University, Colchester, was recorded by the BBC and shown on television as part of the weekly *Rock Goes to College* series. Chris Rea long treasured his happy memories of the tour. His one regret was that he never had the chance to sit and drink all night with Alan, whom he called 'as talented as any of the American league of that time and in the Grand Prix of Formula 1 songwriters'.[8]

There were to be six Christmas shows at Newcastle that December, including another charity event. At a children's show for over 2,000 disabled youngsters, organised with the Variety Club of Great Britain, they were not only entertained to a concert from the group but also given presents, ice creams, sweets, cokes, crisps, and, naturally, party hats. This rapidly became part of the tradition, and every year, an afternoon benefit gig was arranged, during which the area around the City Hall would be almost blocked by special buses and Variety Club Sunshine coaches—to say nothing of the heart-warming sight of large numbers of children in wheelchairs being helped into the building. As for the regular shows that year, there were a few surprises for the audience. When the Killingworth sword dancers came on stage dressed as greasers, they were serenaded with a few bars from 'Summer Nights', the John Travolta and Olivia Newton-John hit from *Grease*, which then segued into 'We Can Swing Together', while during Chris Rea's set, Ray and Rod made a brief appearance dressed as ice cream ladies. Even the group were astonished at one point when Jacka did an impersonation onstage, complete with his own sound effects, of Sir Douglas Bader baling out of a Spitfire—and then looked up to see model airmen dropping from the hall ceiling on miniature parachutes.

Early in 1979, the group flew out to Australia and New Zealand for a series of about eight planned shows to be staged throughout February. The one in Auckland, it was assumed, would make the most money and subsidise the remainder, but it had to be postponed due to a typhoon and rescheduled for four days later. The only date on which they could play it coincided with the equivalent of Independence Day. Although the rearranged show was given plenty of publicity, only about 500 came instead of the hoped-for 8,000. Everyone who came enjoyed themselves, but as the group could not afford to finance the rest of the tour themselves, the remaining dates had to be cancelled.

At around the same time, 'Warm Feeling', one of the two Jackson-Harcourt songs on *Back and Fourth*, slipped out as a single at home, but disappointing reviews and lack of airplay stifled any chances of success. An appearance on television's *Cheggers Plays Pop* in April, six weeks after release, failed to boost its chances.

Early that summer, Rocket issued *Phantoms*, another Alan solo album, and like *Pipedream*, with another painting by Magritte, *Le musée du roi*, on the front cover. It was in effect a partial reissue of the Radiator album, with six songs from the former being used, alongside an alternative version of 'Make Me Want to Stay' from *Back and Fourth*, and with Alan and Mickey Sweeney credited as co-producers. Two of the songs, 'A Walk in the Sea' and 'Madmen and Loonies', would appear regularly in the Lindisfarne set onstage. It suggested that Alan was reluctant to lay his solo career aside, just because the group had reformed.

Although they had hoped to use Gus Dudgeon again as producer for their next studio album, he was unavailable and Hugh Murphy came on board instead. This time the venue was Chipping Norton Studios, where Hugh had just produced two successive top ten albums for Gerry Rafferty. To supplement the seven new songs by Alan were two from Rod, one from Jacka and Charlie, and one from Si. The latter's contribution, 'Dedicated Hound', was singled out for particular praise, ironically not least by the press, although it was a scarcely-veiled attack on music journalists: 'I don't need to hear your guitar—I'll write my review from the bar, should go far'. The group had been augmented on the sessions by keyboard player

Pete Wingfield, plus a brass arrangement on one track from Nick Rowley, and strings on three songs from Graham Preskett. One of the songs to benefit from the latter, 'Good To Be Here?', was regarded as one of Alan's most thought-provoking lyrics, an epic number about a peculiar dream he once had.

The album was due for release in September. A few weeks earlier, when Si and members of Dire Straits were sitting around, chatting, and wondering what to call their respective groups' forthcoming albums, Pick Withers had suggested that Straits' second, which was due for release in June, should be *The News*. Mark Knopfler said he liked the idea, but thought *Communiqué* might be better. Pick said he thought *The News* sounded more direct, but Mark's choice was preferred and ultimately adopted. When Si told the rest of Lindisfarne about it, they agreed that *The News* sounded good—and the choice was made.

Although *The News* was regarded as another worthy album, none of the tracks on it caught the public or indeed the media's collective ear as 'Run for Home' had. It spawned two singles, both written by Alan, 'Easy and Free' and 'Call of the Wild', the latter with Rod's prominent fiddle playing being as close as the album got to the folk-rock style that they had personified in their early days. Yet chart success proved sorely lacking this time round. Despite this, it was always Jacka's favourite album by the group because, in his view, it had a good mix of styles, encompassing the best use of their musicianship and writing talent: 'I think the band were at their most inventive and probably at their peak as a five-piece unit around this period'.[9]

A further disappointment came with news from across the Atlantic. 'Run for Home' and *Back and Fourth*, both released in America by Atco Records, had sold well and received good reviews. Those who found the album a little too easy listening and wondered if it had been made with an eye on the American market had probably hit the nail on the head, with Barry McKay saying quite openly that he would like to see the group make it big in the international markets. Rough and ready Tyneside folk songs were clearly not the way to court audiences stateside. Another American tour, which would have doubtless been more successful than the miserable affair of their last one six years previously, had been pencilled in for the summer. Then, several members of staff at Atco left, and those who joined the company in their place rejected *The News*, so the tour was cancelled. Barry had planned for them to arrive in the States 'in style', travelling in a large bus and staying in the best hotels, but with the sudden loss of record company support, it would not be cost-effective.

According to Ray—who had probably the best business head among them and would later combine his drumming duties with that of being their manager—when they reformed, the group had made it an unwritten rule that, after what happened more than once the first time round, they would never embark on anything else on which they would knowingly lose money. Going abroad to play on a small budget and breaking even would be acceptable, but this could not be guaranteed without proper backing. The cold wind of a financial recession was starting to bite the music industry. Record companies on both sides of the Atlantic were becoming more cost-conscious than in the halcyon days, when a few major hits helped to bankroll large advances while accepting that some of their less successful or less fashionable signings might not come anywhere near recouping the initial outlay.

Given such circumstances, Jacka was fortunate in being given free rein, if briefly, to launch the solo career under Phonogram that had been aborted on EMI four years previously. After *The News* was released, he had another look at the demos already recorded. Keen to ensure it would not sound just like another Lindisfarne album and wanting to explore his love of soul and blues, he and Hugh Murphy assembled a set of session musicians including guitarist Steve Lipson—who also engineered the album (as he had *The News*)—Pete Wingfield, and Betsy Cook (Steve's wife) on keyboards, DeLisle Harper (bass guitarist from Gonzalez), and Charlie Harcourt and Micky Moody on guitars. Six songs came from the demos written with Charlie, but Phonogram asked him and Hugh to compromise and omit some of the original material they had hoped to include, in order to use songs from other sources and make it sound more commercial. Among the additional numbers recorded were Sam Cooke's 'You Send Me', a long-time favourite of his, a ballad-style rearrangement of 'In the Midnight Hour', and the Stealers Wheel hit 'Everything Will Turn Out Fine', on which co-writer Gerry Rafferty contributed backing vocals. Many years later, Ray said he enjoyed making the album, but it had come a little too late as music trends were moving on and he felt it sounded slightly old-fashioned by the time it was finished. At the record company's request, one song included was a cover version of 'Little Town Flirt', which everyone regarded as a potential hit single if only it would get the breaks.

Yet neither this nor the title track, which were released as 45s during the first few weeks of 1980, made any headway, while the album *In the Night* only sold about 150 copies. Steve Lipson dismissed it as 'candy floss', while the record label head of A&R, Rodger Bain, was equally unenthusiastic. All the same, Jacka said later that of the many producers he had worked with, Steve was the most creative, being a very good musician and engineer, and meticulous in choosing the right chords if he thought one fitted better than what was on offer. Gus Dudgeon was a close second, *Back and Fourth* being beautifully recorded and giving them what he thought was their most commercial-sounding album.

With one failed solo album and one under-performing group set, Lindisfarne and Phonogram Records parted company. Having weathered so many ups and downs, they were not unduly bothered by the lack of a record contract. In the early 1980s, the day of reckoning was about to come for each major British record company in one way or another. Acts who had been strong sellers three or four years before were learning that in the show business world nothing stood still, fans could be fickle, and after one or two flops in a row, they could expect to be shown the door. On the other hand, small independent record labels with similarly reduced overheads to match were proving that there was another way to get their product into the shops, and even occasionally into the Top 10 as well.

Lindisfarne remained in demand for programmes on television at home and abroad, as well as playing gigs up and down the land as if determined to demonstrate that they played all the year round, not only at Newcastle during the festive season. They too would soon go along the indie records route. In April, shortly after the release of *In the Night*, they returned to Chipping Norton Studios with Steve Lipson for further recordings. The first to see the light of day, Alan's 'Friday Girl', came out that summer on their own Subterranean label through the independent Spartan Records. It was one of the songs in their set when they played Knebworth Festival on 21 June with The Beach Boys, Santana, The Blues Band, and Mike Oldfield, and again at another festival, Loch Lomond, at Balloch Park the following day. For the next few months, they were busy on the live circuit, playing shows in Europe, as well as a benefit in August at Alnwick Playhouse for the Cheviot Defence Action Group, campaigning against the storage of nuclear waste in the area, at which they shared a bill with Michael Chapman and jammed with him on three songs.

Another single also recorded at Chipping Norton, 'Red Square Dance', was released soon afterwards, credited to The Defectors. Originally submitted as a theme to the Moscow Olympics on the suggestion of Brendan Foster, County Durham-born long-distance runner and bronze medal-winner in the 1976 Olympics, it was completed just as Russia invaded Afghanistan. Sometimes known by the band as 'The Dog Tune', it became a regular live favourite and for some years they used it to open the second half of their shows.

After a couple more days of recording in Surrey Sound Studios in October, the group prepared for their next round of shows at Newcastle City Hall. One of the performances just before Christmas was for the Variety Club to a crowd of 2,500 children. The seasonal shows comprised eleven dates altogether, during which they played to 28,000 people.

Most of the year 1981 was spent on the road. It started with a week of London club and pub dates in January where they played the Marquee, the Greyhound in Fulham, the Tramshed in Woolwich, the Half Moon in Putney, the Venue, and Dingwalls. Next on the itinerary were college and university gigs alongside larger concert halls. March and April were spent rehearsing new material, returning to Chipping Norton Studios with Steve, and three weeks of recording and mixing followed.

There were two major festivals during the summer. In July, they were part of Lisdoonvarna, a three-day event at County Clare, Ireland, alongside Chris de Burgh and his Band, Paul Brady, Planxty, Steel Pulse, and The Beat. During the last weekend of August, they were special guests at Rock on the Tyne and the International Stadium, Gateshead, with Dr Feelgood, Rory Gallagher, Elvis Costello and the Attractions, the still relatively new and unknown U2, and Ian Dury and The Blockheads, whose line-up included Alan's former colleagues in The Chosen Few and Skip Bifferty, Johnny Turnbull and Mickey Gallagher. Once again, the year was rounded off by Newcastle City Hall shows at Christmas, which were fast becoming more or less an annual institution.

Only one new Lindisfarne record appeared in 1981. 'I Must Stop Going to Parties', as the title hinted, was a song by Alan that came close to novelty territory. Backed by Si's 'See How They Run', a number that would have probably appeared on Jack the Lad's last album were it not for his departure, it took the joke further by coming out on the Hangover label. As an effort to take advantage of the regular demand for comedy records in the Christmas chart, it failed.

Early in 1982, the group hit the live circuit again, appearing in a slightly unusual guise, as part of Pacamax. Rod had previously said he would welcome the idea of being in a slightly looser aggregation, and Pacamax was just that—a revolving door of Tyneside musicians, getting together for fun. Among the personnel were most of Lindisfarne, plus Brendan Healy from the Eastside Torpedoes on keyboards, Billy Mitchell from Jack the Lad, Jed Grimes from Hedgehog Pie on guitar, and saxophonist Marty Craggs from Harcourt's Heroes, who had continued for a few more months without Jacka before disbanding in June 1978. Their repertoire was drawn from songs from various favourite artists of theirs, such as Warren Zevon's 'Lawyers, Guns and Money' and Steve Earle's 'The Devil's Right Hand'.

Much of the rest of 1982 was taken up with more festival appearances during the summer, including a headlining slot at Roskilde, Denmark, in June, and Macroom, Munster, Ireland, in July, alongside The Chieftains and Roy Harper. In August, they shared top billing with Joan Baez at the Cambridge Folk Festival, finishing a well-received set on a very hot afternoon by getting the crowd on their feet to join in with 'We Can Swing Together'. Next on their itinerary was the Theakston Music Festival at Nostell Priory, near Wakefield, alongside The Blues Band, Ralph McTell, and Jethro Tull, now including Dave Pegg, formerly with Fairport Convention, on bass guitar. At the backstage bar, Dave's nose was on the receiving end of a punch from Alan, although it was admittedly harmless. Nobody really knew why, but it was said to have been an inebriated Alan's desire to settle an old score, remembering an occasion some years previously when both groups had shared a bill at Manchester and enjoyed a curry together afterwards. Fairport had left in a hurry, leaving the Geordies to pick up the tab.

Alan himself had suffered rather more in a separate incident around that time, being admitted to hospital with a punctured lung sustained after a game of football. It had delayed the already protracted recording sessions that had continued unhurried over the last two years or so. Although the working title had been *Party Politics*, the album that surfaced as *Sleepless Nights*, the debut on their own label, LMP (Lindisfarne Musical Productions), produced by Steve Lipson, was released in October. Despite his withering opinion of *In the Night*, Jacka liked and respected Steve for his excellent musical ear, talent as a guitarist and apparent knowledge of every gizmo around at that time. Steve, he said, impressed on them that they needed to modernise their sound, and to this end encouraged them to buy and use a synth to record with. It gave *Sleepless Nights* a completely new dimension, he said, but without taking away their traditional sound: 'I thought the songs on the album were well recorded and performed, I felt it was quite strong overall'.[10]

Ray thought *Sleepless Nights* was a bit of a transitional album for them. As a great guitar player and the first producer they worked with who was also a musician, Steve was prepared to take the creative process further than they had been used to:

[He] often spent the evening editing takes (the old analogue method with a razor blade) and presented us with new arrangements of tunes the next morning. He also left a two-track machine running throughout every session as he maintained that the bits that musicians play between takes were often the most creative thing they did. He trawled through those tapes for snippets that could be worked up into new song ideas.[11]

The ten songs on the album from Alan included two of his angriest political numbers to date. 'Cruising to Disaster' railed at President Reagan in the White House on Capitol Hill, 'a fortress to freedom with a license to kill', and at the old men in the Kremlin, while 'Stormy Weather' laid savagely into the threat to peace posed by the build-up of cruise missiles. Balancing them were 'Nights', a doo-wop, fifties-flavoured ballad with Jacka on lead vocal, which was also released as a single, and the previous year's 45 'I Must Stop Going to Parties'. Rod and the Jackson/Harcourt partnership were allotted one each, the former with 'Sunderland Boys' and the latter with 'Learning the Game'. With the handicap of being an independent release, it still sold enough to peak at an entry position of No. 59 on the album chart. The group undertook all marketing and promotion, but could not provide the finance needed to continue plugging it for more than a few weeks; as a result, it fell out of the listings after three weeks.

The record caused some controversy as a result of the politically incorrect sleeve design, being a photograph, not of the group, but of a female model as nature intended, at Wallington Hall, a National Trust property near Morpeth. Its satire on the rock 'n' roll cliché of hedonism and staying up all night went over the heads of the Methodist family who had recently purchased the property, and they rang the group's office to complain. Rod was the one nearest the phone when they called, and in their defence, he pointed out that he had seen several paintings of nude women on the walls while the photoshoot was being arranged.

The year finished with a twenty-nine-date British tour, beginning in Liverpool and culminating in ten nights at Newcastle City Hall. While on the road, they were at last awarded a platinum disc to mark 300,000 sales in Britain of *Fog on the Tyne*.

By now, all the members of Lindisfarne were diversifying into looser conglomerations, working with other artists while keeping the group name alive. It was symptomatic of the way that other established groups were working at the time. Rod had previously expressed discontent with working exclusively with a group, enjoying the freedom of freelancing with various solo artists whom he had long respected. Now he and the others had the best of both worlds. He and Ray worked as part of a house band for Mike Elliott who was presenting a TV series, *At Last It's Mike Elliott*, for Tyne Tees and Channel 4, the revolving door of musicians in effect being those who played together as Pacamax. Ray was playing gigs with folk duo Bob Fox and Stu Luckley, the latter having previously played bass guitar with Hedgehog Pie, after which he and Rod joined Michael Chapman for a radio session in Manchester.

Alan appeared with Pacamax at the Leeds Festival in September, also playing his own set featuring material from another solo album, *On the Other Side*, co-produced again by him and Mickey Sweeney. The musicians who accompanied him on the album—Pete Kirtley on guitar, Frank Gibbon on bass guitar, and Paul Smith on drums—were his group at the festival. Events in the South Atlantic the previous year had fuelled his anger, which burst forth in another anti-war song, 'Malvinas Melody', which made clear his feelings on the Falklands conflict. Like 'Poor Old Ireland', it was banned by the BBC, but such a restriction was more or less academic as, by this time, any new material from Alan had little chance of finding its way onto the Radio 1 and 2 playlists. Another song that would remain part of Alan's repertoire, as well as that of Lindisfarne as a group, was 'Day of the Jackal', his comment on the state of Middle East affairs.

When Alan joined the Labour Party in 1980, the only surprise was that he had not done so years before. There was a suggestion that the Transport & General Workers' Union and the National Union of Mineworkers would sponsor him to run for Parliament, in which case he could be more or less guaranteed a safe seat— he considered the idea. It would certainly have been an unusual situation for one of Britain's leading songwriters to hold down a career as performer and musician while simultaneously taking his place on the green benches at Westminster. During the year-long miners' strike, which began in the spring of 1984, he was part of the Red Wedge project, appearing live at benefit gigs at Newcastle City Hall with Billy Bragg and Paul Weller, two of the musicians most noted as activists at the time. He served as secretary of his local constituency branch at Whickham, performed in Blackpool during the party conference in 1990, and was always ready to play at concerts on behalf of striking or redundant miners and shipyard workers. In Jacka's words:

> Alan was not just any old pop music writer. He recorded the zeitgeist of the working people of Newcastle, pointing out injustices suffered by ordinary people, exposing those who were to blame. He was a champion of the underdog and latterly became interested in politics to fight for rights at a local level.[12]

Meanwhile, the group continued to demo songs from time to time for another album, although as had been the case with *Sleepless Nights*, relishing the lack of pressure from a record label to complete everything to a deadline. It fitted in with their less rigid schedule and enjoyment of working with other musicians instead of having to focus on being full-time members of Lindisfarne. Alan had recently met Steve Daggett, keyboard player and guitarist with the recently disbanded Stiletto. He was running a studio in Gosforth, and the connection resulted initially in his recording demos for the group and Alan as a soloist, and then playing synthesiser for Alan on a TV performance. From there, it was only a short step to Steve joining the group for a while on keyboards.

The group was expanding to a six-piece, with Marty Craggs playing saxophone, flute, and keyboards as the occasion demanded. After he had done several festivals and tours with them, it came to the stage when they said to him one day that he was with them all the time—'why don't you join?' At first, he was a little apprehensive about being accepted by fans alongside the original members, but he need not have worried. Musically and socially, it proved to be a perfect move for them all.

On 5 July 1984, the group achieved something of an ambition when they appeared at St James' Park, Newcastle, on a bill supporting Bob Dylan and Santana. The two latter acts had been touring Europe that summer, and the Newcastle date was the last. They 'wangled' themselves on the bill, said Ray, because they had heard tickets were not selling very well: 'We contacted the promoter and said we'll guarantee you another 10,000 ticket sales if you put us on. And we did!'[13] Before going on and playing to a crowd of 30,000 fans, Alan and Jacka spoke briefly to a television reporter as they paid tribute to the performer who had long been one of their idols, the man whom they were so looking forward to seeing play later that day, who had 'laid down a lot of the bedrock of rock 'n' roll as it is now', and alongside The Beatles and The Rolling Stones had been one of their formative influences. They never got to meet him as he was surrounded by guards, but they had a great day with marvellous weather, on the 'hallowed turf' where they went down very well.

During the mid-1980s, the music scene was dominated for a while by the reverberations of Band Aid, the charity collective founded by Bob Geldof and Midge Ure to alleviate the effects of famine in Africa. In the wake of their 1984 Christmas single 'Do They Know It's Christmas' and the Live Aid concerts of July 1985, several similar projects followed. Geordie Aid, a collective drawn from over thirty local acts including members of Lindisfarne, John Miles, Brian Johnson of AC/DC, Olga of The Toy Dolls, and Irene Hume of Prelude, were among those who came together at Impulse Studios, Wallsend, to record 'Try Giving Everything', written specially by Mike Waller, former keyboard player with Harcourt's Heroes. Ray said that the aim was 'hopefully going to embarrass governments into realising that things can be done if people want them to'.[14]

That same year, a certain major record company had also suffered some embarrassment. In March 1985, Jacka, supported by Barry McKay, appeared in the High Court defending an action against EMI Records that he claimed had ruined his solo career. Justice Michael Davies said the company had not given him 'a fair crack of the whip' in promoting his records when they had signed him in 1975. Only one single from the contracted three had been released. In their defence, EMI stated that 'Take Some Time' had sold only 300 copies, that musical material provided by him was not satisfactory, and that it would have been a commercial failure. The judge ruled that under the terms of the contract, Mr Jackson had not been obliged to provide his own material. In summing up, he said EMI had failed to fulfil its contracts or demonstrate a legal justification in law or fact for not doing so. He therefore awarded the plaintiff and his manager damages of £12,500 plus interest from January 1978—a total of £23,304.[15]

Steve Daggett was largely the catalyst for Lindisfarne's second album of the eighties. A new record label formed by the group, River City Records, and a marketing and distribution deal with RCA/Ariola, gave purchasers a chance to win accommodation for an overseas holiday; it also provided the banner for the release of *Dance Your Life Away*, released in autumn 1986, and the group's first to appear on compact disc as well as album and cassette. With Steve's keyboards and drum programming dominating the sound throughout, to say nothing of the first word in the title, it showed that the group were as capable as anyone else of keeping up with contemporary trends. 'Shine On' was co-written by Alan and Steve, while apart from Rod's 'Love on the Run', everything else was written by Alan. He maintained that nearly all of them could be performed easily on stage. When they began recording, he and Steve were given a brief by the others to create an album of songs that would work well live.

'Shine On', with its optimistic message and chiming synths, was launched as the perfect Christmas single and backed by some as a possible outsider for a festive chart-topper, though it never charted. There was a similar feel to 'All in the Same Boat', which its writer called 'a nice sort of summery kind of song, nice and easy' with a message of optimism: 'We're living in a troubled world here—we're in it together, so let's try and work together'. Of his other songs, the most lyrically powerful was 'Heroes', written with the miners in mind, but equally applicable to any band of people standing up for their rights. He had wanted to write a song about the strike of 1984–5 and dedicate it to the National Union of Mineworkers. While it did not actually mention the miners, it could have been about any group of people struggling for their rights. 'Take Your Time' was inspired by his daughter, Berenice, then a teenager going through the adolescent pains that everyone does: '[It was] a sort of message to her and her friends. A lot of things look odd and weird and you think that people don't like you and you come to hate the things you really love. If you take the time you come out all right at the other end'. '100 Miles to Liverpool' had its origins in regular letters from two southern fans, which for him started off a train of thought about being on the road for the next tour, with its usual varied emotions—boredom, happiness, and joy on the stage, nostalgia for the places they had been to and what they used to be.

The touring that followed included the customary Christmas shows. Steve proved an asset on stage, putting a contemporary sheen on their sound, playing guitar, 'as well as all the computers and stuff us old chaps don't understand!', as Ray put it.

Due to Lindisfarne's enduring live appeal, this time they made a decision to record a live album with a difference. Fans ordered the album when they bought their tickets, sent in the vouchers, and were promised the record, *Lindisfarntastic!* in January. Having recorded the shows, they were left with so much material that was not used for the first album that *Lindisfarntastic! Volume Two* came a year later.

Yet to survive in an unforgiving business that could be ruthless towards those who took part in it involved taking risks. The group could have remained frozen in aspic, staying in their comfort zone and continuing to record and play live with a repertoire drawn mostly from the hit singles and albums; however, they could also have seized any opportunities as they arose and ran the risk of upsetting some of the more long-established fans who might be averse to anything new or the feeling that 'their band' had leapt on the bandwagon. In certain quarters, the hi-tech gloss of *Dance Your Life Away* had been a little hard to stomach, and the next venture would also run the risk of alienating followers.

In 1987, they were asked to record a TV-promoted party album for Stylus Music, consisting largely of cover versions of old rock 'n' roll numbers. Barry McKay, who had largely relinquished the reins of management and handed over to Ray, thought it was an excellent idea. Any group was an expensive proposition to keep in existence, and as they admitted, they were 'offered a financial lifeline'. However, when given the opportunity to record their own versions, they could hardly resist, the initial idea being to make it their equivalent of The Band's *Moondog Matinee*, said Rod: 'How wrong we were!'[16] As they had grown up with these songs in their DNA, it was something that could be a great deal of fun, and each of them put forward their own suggestions as to what ought to be included. Three sides of the double album were to be oldies from the '50s and '60s, some sequenced and others played as standalone numbers. They included 'Party Doll' (also issued as a single), 'You Never Can Tell, 'Runaround Sue', 'Love You More Than I Can Say', a suitably frenzied 'Keep A'Knockin'', and a segue of 'Let's Dance' and 'New Orleans'.

As the re-recording restrictions on their back catalogue had expired, they devoted one side of the album to six of their old numbers in order to help produce royalties for the writers in the band. 'Meet Me on the Corner', which held faithfully to the original, could hardly be omitted, and 'Fog on the Tyne' was now given a Bo Diddley-style makeover in keeping with the way they had been playing it on stage. 'Run for Home' was embellished with an electronic snare drum track that ironed out the tempo to give the impression it was faster, although Jacka was not too keen on it as he thought it lacked the atmosphere of the original. 'Warm Feeling' now had a slightly reggae feel that they felt worked out sympathetically, and they used the same arrangement when playing it on tour for the next few months. 'Clear White Light', rearranged by Steve Daggett, turned out better than the original in their view. Even so, with hindsight, the re-recording of these songs in a more contemporary vein was a big mistake.

In spite of that, all of them thoroughly enjoyed making the album. They worked on their choices as close to the original versions as possible, analysing the arrangements of the instruments to achieve an authentic sound, and shared the vocals out among themselves to suit the songs. Si, who was now increasingly playing keyboards on stage and in the studio as well as lead guitar, found 'that daft record' particularly entertaining to do, 'recreating the old cheesy organs and violin triddles'. He suggested they should call it *Teddy Boy's Picnic*, but the record company disagreed, and it became *C'mon Everybody* instead. They were by no means the first established act to undertake such a venture. Slade had had some success two years earlier with the festive *Crackers* album, mixing party hits and re-recordings of their earlier hits, while John Lennon and Paul McCartney had both recorded albums of rock 'n' roll standards as soloists in their post-Beatle days.

Yet neither of the Fab Four had been in thrall to a record company that had total control over design of the record as well as distribution. Packaged with a front cover photo of revellers, courtesy of Club 18-30, something the group could obviously do nothing about, it was guaranteed to make even the most faithful fan blench. Reminiscing on the venture as a whole, Steve Daggett called the record 'a fair move' financially speaking, 'but credibility wise, not so good'. He stated: '[The cover photograph was] the final nail in the coffin.... You really should have been in the Lindisfarne office the day the finished product arrived, it was pure Spinal Tap—head in hands hilarity!'[17] Rod agreed: 'The artwork was completely out of our hands, and the finished product was awful'.[18] Rock reference books would throw any neutral point of view stance to the four winds and call the album a new low for the group. Even *The Times*, in an obituary for Alan Hull eight years later, would opine that in recording and releasing it, they 'plummeted to an artistic nadir'.[19] Through television advertising it sold an estimated 60,000 copies, though never quite making the charts, but it ran the risk of incurring the bewilderment of long-term fans for short-term gain. Yet it was not something to be regretted, and that year at the Christmas shows, they allowed themselves the luxury of supporting themselves as a rock 'n' roll act playing the oldies.

More in keeping with preconceptions of the group's roots was the involvement of two of them in another, less heavily advertised project that year. *Woody Lives!* was a tribute to Woody Guthrie, conceived and produced by their friend Geoff Heslop. Rod and Jacka both contributed instruments and vocals to an album of nine songs by Woody, including 'Will You Miss Me' and 'Hard Travellin'', alongside Bert Jansch, Rab Noakes, Dick Gaughan, and others. A share of profits was allocated to the Association to Combat Huntingdon's Chorea, the disease that had claimed his life in middle age.

Another interesting trip down memory lane was a one-off reunion of Downtown Faction. In the autumn of 1987, Jacka, Si, Rod, Ray, and Jeff Sadler convened for the first time in almost twenty years to record a one-off radio appearance for Paul Jones' *Rhythm 'n' Blues* show on BBC Radio 2, broadcast on 1 October. Several tracks were laid down, among them 'Sporting Life Blues' and 'Loving Around the Clock'. Paul, the former frontman of Manfred Mann at the height of the beat boom and long renowned as a presenter, broadcaster, and one of the most respected of blues harmonica players himself, took the opportunity to praise Jacka's prowess on the same instrument.

Rod was spending a certain amount of time working with Bert Jansch, who had recorded four albums with Charisma after Pentangle disbanded in 1973, and had been involved in their reforming a few years later. Bert had had a severe drinking problem, and had given it up after being hospitalised in 1987. After he was discharged, Rod formed a duo with him, resulting in an album, *Leather Launderette*, on which they shared vocals, with Bert contributing guitar and banjo, Rod electric and acoustic guitars, bass guitar, and mandolin, plus Marty Craggs on backing vocals. Bert's biographer Colin Harper called it 'an upbeat, enjoyable but essentially unambitious Rod Clements record with Bert Jansch guesting prominently'. To promote it, they undertook a thirty-one-date tour as a duo in March and April 1988, at which Rod was encouraged by good and appreciative audiences. Although he thought it was good tour, he felt that Bert did not really enjoy the experience very much as he had only just given up drinking and was still convalescent. They drove for several hundred miles on the tour 'and he didn't say much'.[20] Later in the year, Rod joined Pentangle with Bert and they undertook a tour of Britain, Italy, and America. Rod appreciated the experience and was pleased with the album *So Early in the Spring*, which they recorded together, but he felt that 'it was just struggling against the earlier identity'.[21]

It would shortly be a time for Lindisfarne to look back at their past in a major way. Virgin Records had now acquired the complete Charisma catalogue, and in 1988, the subject of reissuing their first three albums on compact disc arose. Although they were happy to endorse the inclusion of the non-album B-sides of the singles as additional tracks,

The Chosen Few, Alan Hull's first group, 1965, from an advertisement for Hohner instruments.

Left: Downtown Faction, *c.* 1967.
Left to right: Don Whittaker; Ray Laidlaw; Richard Squirrel; and Rod Clements. (*Richard Squirrel*)

Lindisfarne, early summer 1972. Another picture from the same session appeared on a poster included with *Dingly Dell*. (*Ronald Pearse Images*)

Lindisfarne at the Crystal Palace Bowl, September 1972, where they shared a bill with Yes and the Mahavishnu Orchestra. (*Croydon Music Archive*)

Alan Hull.
(*Croydon*
Music Archive)

Ray Jackson. (*Croydon Music Archive*)

Rod Clements. (*Croydon Music Archive*)

Above left: Si Cowe. (*Croydon Music Archive*)

Above right: Ray Laidlaw. (*Croydon Music Archive*)

Above: Rab Noakes.
(*Ronald Pearse Images*)

Right: The imminent
announcement of
Lindisfarne's split, from
the front of *New Musical
Express*, 31 March 1973.

Jack the Lad, 1973. *Left to right*: Billy Mitchell; Ray Laidlaw; Rod Clements; and Si Cowe.

Lindisfarne at the Reading Festival, August 1973. From the cover of the *Roll On, Ruby* songbook. *Left to right*: Paul Nichols; Tommy Duffy; Ray Jackson; Charlie Harcourt; Alan Hull; and Kenny Craddock.

Lindisfarne, 1974, shortly before they disbanded.

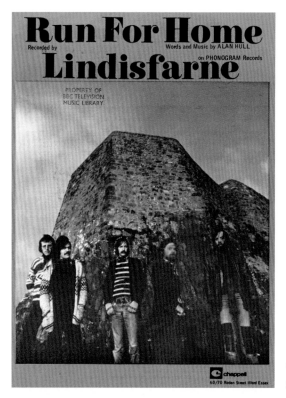

'Run for Home', the British sheet music.

'Run for Home', the American sheet music.

A promotional picture of Lindisfarne at the time of *The News*, 1979.

Lindisfarne at the Duke of Wellington, Newcastle-upon-Tyne, *c*. 1982.

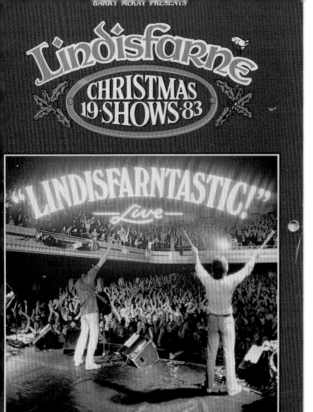

BARRY McKAY PRESENTS

Lindisfarne
CHRISTMAS 19·SHOWS·83

"LINDISFARNTASTIC!"
—Live—

56 Page BUMPER EDITION
includes Full Colour 1984 Calendar

Left: The programme for Lindisfarne's 1983 Christmas shows, which also doubled as a 1984 calendar.

Below: Lindisfarne at the Hammersmith Odeon, January 1987, with newest member Marty Craggs on saxophone. (*Alison Baker*)

The sleeve for 'Party Doll', the single from *C'mon Everybody*, reproducing the unloved Club 18-30 design, 1987.

Lindisfarne (the group) run for home to Lindisfarne (the island), 1988.

Lindisfarne, 1988.

Gazza (Paul Gascoigne), third from right, and Lindisfarne at the time of 'Fog on the Tyne (Revisited)', 1990. Behind him on his left, new bass guitarist Steve Cunningham.

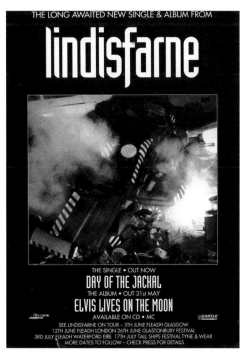

A promotional flyer for *Elvis Lives on the Moon*, 1993.

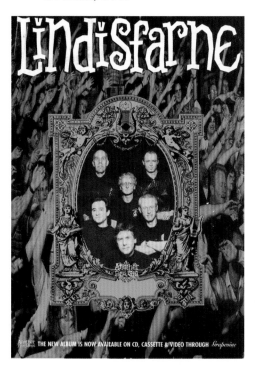

Above left: A flyer for Lindisfarne's return in 1996, including new members Billy Mitchell, Dave Hull-Denholm, and Ian Thomson, promoting the live album *Another Fine Mess*, recorded on their twenty-fifth anniversary the previous year.

Above right: A flyer for the 1998–1999 concert tour, promoting *Here Comes the Neighbourhood*.

Above left: Rod Clements, *c.* 2000.

Above right: Billy Mitchell, *c.* 2000.

The memorial plaque to Alan Hull, Newcastle City Hall. (*Derek Walmsley*)

Above: Ray Jackson's Lindisfarne on stage at Newcastle City Hall, December 2013. (*Derek Walmsley*)

Below: Ray Jackson's Lindisfarne on stage at Newcastle City Hall, December 2014. (*Derek Walmsley*)

Above: Rod Clements's Lindisfarne on stage at Masham Town Hall, the first concert with Rod fronting the group, May 2015. (*Derek Walmsley*)

Below: Rod Clements's Lindisfarne on stage at Newcastle City Hall, December 2015. (*Derek Walmsley*)

the group declined an offer to remix them on the grounds that they wanted the original recordings to be heard as they were completed at the time. They participated in a set of new photoshoots on Holy Island, and for a genuine picture to adorn the front of *Dingly Dell*, thus banishing the old sepia cardboard sleeve that had caused such grief the first time round. It coincided with a retread of 'Lady Eleanor', from the *C'Mon Everybody* sessions, produced by Steve Daggett and issued as a single. Also in the record shops at the same time was a four-track EP, *The Peel Sessions*, containing material recorded for the BBC and first broadcast in 1972.

A new single also appeared, in the name of another worthy cause. It was revealed that Elders, the Australian brewery, had bid £1.6 billion for Scottish & Newcastle Breweries, a takeover bid that, if completed, would almost certainly sound the death knell for many local jobs. As Alan underlined when speaking to the press, the city could ill afford any such rise in unemployment. While he was sitting on the lavatory one day, he came up with the idea for another song, 'Save Our Ales'. When it was pressed, the run-out groove of the record featured an inscription from the cutting engineer George Peckham, 'Dog bites Skippy', 'dog' being the local name for Newcastle Brown Ale. The single was not a hit, but Scottish & Newcastle successfully fought off the bid.

Among the live dates the group played towards the end of 1988— including the now more or less obligatory five nights at Newcastle City Hall—and first months of 1989, at home and overseas, were a few shows in Italy. That February, while sitting in a café (which sold beer as well as espresso) in Milan—where they had been booked to play for a week in a club, giving them the chance to get away and spend some time together without having to travel every day—the group decided on a return to their roots. After the more (perhaps too much so) contemporary sounding *Dance Your Life Away* and *C'mon Everybody*, which had appalled some of the faithful, there was a growing feeling, both inside and well beyond the band, that they were getting way too far away from what had always distinguished them as Lindisfarne.

In short, it would be to write and record a new album of songs that they could play on stage without gimmicks; in their words, 'let's pack the record with belters'. With this in mind, they went into Reeltime Studios, Newcastle, that spring, having resolved to get back to basic principles, write some new songs, and record an album that was more true to the band's character, even if it meant 'scaling things down a bit'. Barry MacKay's tenure as their manager came to an end around the same time, and there was a strong sense of turning over a new leaf and of their being more true to themselves. 'Milan was a bit of a turning point,' said Rod, 'and we came home highly motivated and with a new sense of direction, and *Amigos* was the result.'[22]

Amigos had begun with Steve Daggett as co-producer with the group, but he left in the summer of 1989 part of the way through: '[It had been] personally a very low time in my life and I was fairly exhausted from the daily running of the studio and long hours of engineering duties'. Before his departure, he had recognized that the *Amigos* album was a crucial one for all of them and they needed to recover their form. He suggested that they write some songs together, something they had never attempted previously, and the results were three collaborations: Rod and Alan's 'Working for the Man', Alan and Marty's 'Everything Changes', and Rod and Marty's 'Roll On That Day'. This was the start of a pattern that would carry on throughout their subsequent albums. However, once recording at Reeltime began, he said, he was 'beginning to crumble physically and mentally and after completing five or six tracks [he] had to leave the studio, the band and the album behind'.[23] Mickey Sweeney, by now an old hand, came in to continue from where he had left off.

Issued that autumn on Black Crow, a small independent label specialising in folk and roots music, the new album was seen by fans as a return to form after the over contemporary sounding *Dance Your Life Away*. One of the most impressive songs was Alan's 'One World', a ballad written for the newest member of his family, with an instrumental reprise of the same, 'Another World', featuring Kathryn Tickell on Northumbrian pipes and closing the album. The idea had originally come to him while he was babysitting his six-month old granddaughter Roxanne: 'Thinking about her future and the planet she would be inheriting from us led to the idea of one world. It's optimistic, idealistic, some might say naïve, but I can't wait to do it on stage.'[24]

It was, however, noticeable—as had been the case with the previous album—for a comparative lack of input from Jacka and Si. Jacka, had moved to London with his wife after the death of his mother-in-law in 1987, and was now increasingly marginalised. Rod had meant him to sing on 'Roll On That Day', but as he could not make the session, it was given to Marty instead. Si had likewise moved, although a good deal less further away, and had settled at Thornton-le-Dale on the edge of the Yorkshire Moors. He said he enjoyed writing near water, and had come up with five or six from which to choose for the sessions, but when he played them all at the studio, the general opinion of each one was 'very interesting, but...' As he admitted with a smile, they were 'a little too strange' for the group.

Alan had also released *Another Little Adventure* on Black Crow, a live solo album, with young Tyneside musician Ian McCallum. It was a revisiting of old songs from the group's back catalogue, including 'January

Song' and 'All Fall Down', alongside his own material, giving a new outing to 'Money Game', 'United States of Mind', and 'Dan the Plan', alongside the more politically direct 'Malvinas Melody' and 'Heroes'.

By the time the group went on tour, they had expanded again to a septet. Rod's guest appearances with other artists had generally been on guitar and slide guitar, and he was now relinquishing bass guitar duties to Steve Cunningham. Alan had just broken his ankle and sat behind his piano for most of the time on stage, although it failed to detract from the general musical display from all combined. Several reviewers praised the combination of Si's keyboards and Marty's flute on 'A Walk in the Sea', as well as Alan's acoustic and Rod's slide on 'Winter Song'.

Yet for one of the longest-serving members, the last ride was approaching.

'Ta-ra, bonny lad'

In 1990, the group completed a sponsorship deal with Theakston's Breweries, which was to last for two years. Two bottles of Theakston's had been prominently displayed on the cover of *Sleepless Nights*—almost as conspicuously on the front as the young lady on the back—and it was arranged that the twenty-first anniversary tour would be named the Old Peculier Tour. Twenty-five dates had been scheduled, including two at London's Mean Fiddler, and five at Newcastle City Hall. The Theakston association was to be launched with a media gig at the White Bear, Masham, North Yorkshire.

Unfortunately, it would be remembered mainly for the wrong reasons. For the previous two years, Jacka had been dissatisfied about lack of work with the group. After moving to London, his wife found him a job in public relations work for the Guinness company. Alan was particularly annoyed as a result by what he perceived as Jacka's lack of commitment, and had planned to raise the issue with him.

Jacka was also not completely at ease with Marty's full-time membership of the group, although not for personal reasons. They had played together as members of Harcourt's Heroes prior to Lindisfarne's reunion twelve years earlier, and had great respect for each other's abilities as musicians. In his view, they performed well together integrating sax and harmonica in both bands, but he disagreed with their decision to make Marty an official member, especially as he had never been consulted:

[Marty] had been a hired hand for several tours after we had recorded *Sleepless Nights*, a good addition to capture the feel of some of the recorded arrangements, but only that. We gradually introduced other players to free Rod to play guitar and fiddle but they were never asked to be full members. The five original members, I thought, performed well together and were such a tight unit. We introduced additional instrumentation to beef up the live sound, to be more like the sound on record, but I think in doing so, lost some of our originality in the process.[1]

Jacka also believed that there were important business considerations for keeping the group relatively compact, and that the more of them there were, the less economic it would be. The whole entourage, he felt, became top heavy, and some of their tours began losing money, supporting an ever-increasing cast of personnel and helpers: 'This put pressure on me to find other sources of income, mainly outside of the band and with that, my commitment, and this eventually led to me severing ties'.[2] With no hit singles since 1978 and only one modestly charting album after that, their record sales had diminished. He had found it exceptionally difficult getting any of his compositions on albums, and therefore did not have the songwriting royalties coming in that Alan and, to a lesser extent, Rod did. As they had not recorded any of his songs when they were at their most successful during the first three years, he was not receiving any additional income from publishing and performing royalties. Some groups who had a couple of main songwriters would insist that all income from publishing and writing was distributed equally among each of the members, but this was never the case with Lindisfarne. The result was a disparity of earnings within the group, where one or two were much better off and could survive without performing or could afford to pursue separate projects outside the band. Ironically, 'King's Cross Blues', one of Jacka's collaborations with Charlie Harcourt, had been played live regularly for some years to great acclaim, but had to be dropped from the act after a tragic fire at the London underground station of November 1987 left thirty-one dead and over 100 injured. Basically, he could not really afford to be in a group in which he felt he was no longer playing an important role.

When asked later about his departure from the group, he stressed that being in a band was great fun, particularly when playing to packed houses and selling records. Yet nothing lasts forever, and with reduced record sales and less than half-full gigs, the more mundane aspects of show business hit home with a vengeance. It was very different from being in a regular job with a monthly salary to top up the bank balance, put food on the table, and pay the mortgage and the utilities. Membership of such a group meant that there were long periods when no monies at all were coming in.

Unlike Alan, who had long been pursuing his own musical ventures outside the group, Jacka was not a solo performer as such and needed a band—or at least a couple of backing musicians to perform separately, which was not cost-effective; and unlike Rod, who had worked with Bert Jansch and Pentagle, he had not had the same musical freelance opportunities with others. Not wanting to be a slave to the bank manager from one earning period to the next, he had reluctantly decided to take a seasonal job that would at least cover him financially for part of the year when they had no touring commitments, rather like being an actor 'resting' between parts. As a promotional manager with a sports marketing agency on sporting sponsorships, he was allocated to the Guinness special events team when they sponsored two cars in the British Touring Car Championships. It was initially a ten-month contract, where he was for once receiving regular income and keeping afloat.

This had fitted in neatly with most of Lindisfarne's commitments as a group, which were few in the summer of 1988. However, their fortunes did not improve the following year when they released the *Amigos* album, which never charted, and all costs had to be recouped from the proceeds of their live performances, further depleting their earnings. In effect, he was now subsidising the group as an unpaid session player, performing other writers' songs that failed to generate significant income, spending much time and effort and long periods away from home and family for little or no financial return. Meanwhile, he was offered another season's work with the marketing agency, and was left with little choice but to accept it because of the group's financial circumstances. A pattern was thus established whereby he became less involved with their day-to-day decision making and he was slowly and increasingly being excluded and not consulted over future policy. It did not help that the rest of the group were based in Newcastle while he was living in London. A telephone call to brief him occasionally, he said, would have been appreciated. As he had committed himself to a summer schedule in his new job, he had to miss the odd gig. Something had to give and he was eventually asked to commit to the group or go:[3]

> I could see it coming when Alan asked me to leave the band. I was becoming more and more disillusioned with the fact that we were making albums nobody was buying and I didn't like the direction the band was heading. I just wasn't fulfilling myself any more. I was subsidising the band which was mad, and I couldn't justify playing with them anymore. If we had stuck to the big Christmas reunion shows I might have perhaps stayed with it.[4]

When he and his wife travelled up from London for the Theakston's gig at Masham and he arrived at the soundcheck, he noticed a definite atmosphere. Yet for Alan to seize the opportunity to bring the subject up at a brewery after already taking advantage of the hospitality, as he invariably did in good measure, had plainly been unwise. Telling Jacka he was just 'playing around', he asked bluntly, 'why don't you leave?'⁵ As co-manager as well as drummer, Ray was furious with Alan for having forced the issue so tactlessly. While aware that Alan had had a point, he considered it was the wrong time and the wrong place. Jacka was the injured party, and in a room full of strangers, it had been thoroughly embarrassing for him, if not for them all. If Alan could not guarantee that he would never ever repeat such behaviour, Ray said, he would walk. The only solution was for a meeting and a calm rational discussion.

Another factor had also entered the equation. What had been a difficult decision for Jacka to make was eased by the fact that the others had committed to make a record with Paul Gascoigne. 'Gazza', the footballer and for a while the darling of the celebrity gossip pages, had been a lifelong fan of Lindisfarne. Ray received a phone call from an old friend in London who had signed Gazza up to make a record, just after the 1990 World Cup in Italy when he was at the peak of his popularity. Ray and Alan, the group's football fans, were hugely impressed with his skills as a player, and Lindisfarne were invited to participate on his album. His manager Mel Stein suggested they should re-record instrumental versions of their hits, Gazza would reminisce about boyhood days on Tyneside and they would dub his speech over the music. They said no to that. Alan, Marty and Ray then went for a pint to discuss the possibilities and came up with the idea of rewriting 'Fog on the Tyne' specifically for Gazza. After Alan and Marty had written new lyrics, the group made a demo and sent it to London, where Gazza and his management loved it. Steve Daggett and Steve Cunningham then produced the master instrumental track in Newcastle which Alan and Steve Daggett then took to London to add Gazza's vocal, and the finished track was then remixed by some dance music experts. 'At that point we thought it was an album track but after a few days we were contacted to see if we were happy with it being released as a single and we agreed,' said Ray, 'The rest is history. It was meant to be a bit of fun and a vote of thanks to Gazza for all the pleasure he had given us on the football pitch. Not everyone saw it that way.'⁶

Jacka was the last to hear of it, and all the plans took place without his knowledge. It was presented to him as a way for them to find their way back into the charts, and he was asked to overdub their backing track with a guide vocal in rap style that Gazza could imitate. He felt uncomfortable with the idea and considered it ill-judged on the grounds that it was totally at odds with their reputation, built over the previous two decades of performing and writing. Although caught up with the idea at first, he half-heartedly went along with the recording stage, but he soon realised it was not for him and he refused to take part in the video. He fully understood why the rest of them 'needed this liaison with Gazza from the financial and publicity point of view, but this seemed to colour their vision as far as credibility was concerned'.[7]

They therefore went ahead without his involvement. 'Fog on the Tyne (Revisited)', credited to Gazza and Lindisfarne with Alan and Marty billed as joint writers, was recorded, co-produced by Steve Daggett and Steve Cunningham, released as a single on black vinyl and picture disc, and went straight on to the Radio 1 playlist and TV. A video recorded at Red's Club, Newcastle, owned by Brian Johnson's ex-wife Carol, was shown on *Top of the Pops*. The single entered the charts at No. 11 and peaked at No. 2 the following week, held only at bay by The Righteous Brothers' 'Unchained Melody', a four-week chart-topper just reissued on the strength of its use in the movie *Ghost* and the biggest-selling single in Britain that year. Gazza had a large following and younger fans clearly loved it, but many a long-standing admirer of the group heard it with a sigh. As one journalist summed it up, it was 'a triumph of celebrity over art'.[8]

Yet as Steve Daggett said, at least they were back in the charts. It would have been far worse for them if the record had flopped. Nobody, not even the group themselves, expected it to do that well, especially as other, more high-profile acts had recently made singles with footballers and failed. If a commitment with Tottenham Hotspur had not prevented Gazza from going on *Top of the Pops* in person with them, that coveted No. 1 would probably have been theirs after all: 'The song is legendary all over Britain, if not further. Ask someone to sing you a Geordie song and it's just as likely to be 'Fog on the Tyne' as 'Blaydon Races' or 'Cushy Butterfield''.[9] More than two decades later, the Gazza and Lindisfarne collaboration would still be remembered on *Popmaster* on Ken Bruce's Radio 2 morning show, and in a general knowledge round on BBC television's *Mastermind*.

On behalf of the others, Marty defended the record as a fun thing. While admitting that the group may have lost some credibility, he conceded that 'it was no worse than any other rap song on the radio at the time'.[10] Its main competition in the genre was Vanilla Ice's 'Ice Ice Baby', a record that had sampled Queen & David Bowie's 'Under Pressure' without permission from the original creators, later resulting in an out of court settlement. About two years later, the present author saw a copy of the original *Fog on the Tyne* album in a second-hand record shop, and underneath the price sticker on the sleeve a small label saying 'NO GAZZA'.

In the summer of 1991, the group played live at Trowbridge Village Pump Festival in Wiltshire and Newark Castle, and laid down some more tracks at Hi-Level Recording Studios, Newcastle. It was now over twenty years since they had first got together, and as yet there was no end in sight. Around that time, Rod was asked how long he saw the group lasting:

[He could not] see any reason not to do it. If any of us got tremendously interested in doing something else, then we could always give it a rest, or just get back together at Christmas and do whatever we like the rest of the year, but there's no reason to knock it on the head. We all get on tremendously well with each other, we have done for years. We're not going to fall out now. We understand each other's differences, and we leave space for everybody to have their head. We construct the band's show now to make sure that everybody gets the chance to show off what they're good at.[11]

In November 1991, they visited Russia, playing a benefit for the child victims of Chernobyl at the Minsk Dynamo Stadium. While there, they met up with Bob Young, an old mate from nearly twenty years ago when he had been roadie and harmonica player with Status Quo on the tour down under, and now managing Liverpool group Sian. Even so, the Russian tour was a real eye-opener for them all, with gangs of gypsies and small children living on the streets and sleeping in the subway. Russia in the immediate post-Gorbachev era, said Ray, was a very sobering experience. No western visitor could fail to be moved by what the people had endured and were still going through: 'Here was a nation once so proud reduced to literally scraping a living. They'd won freedom but the structure of their society was crumbling. At least under the communists everyone was fed'.[12]

The show was a great success and quite an emotional occasion. Marty recalled Alan, who had an instant rapport with everyone, jumping into the middle of a five-deep row of soldiers in their late teens with very stern faces, taking the cap off the head of one of them and placing it on his own. None of the Minsk youngsters had ever seen a stadium gig before. While other groups merely played, Marty felt that Lindisfarne 'went out and grabbed the audience' until there were tears in the eyes of the crowd.

After a more convivial stint playing in Hong Kong, the group returned to Britain and back to the studio. At around this time, they acquired a co-manager, Steve Weltman, who would work alongside Ray while serving as the managing director of Charisma, enjoying a new, if brief, lease of life after signing Malcolm McLaren and Julian Lennon to its small but select roster. Strat was no longer part of the picture, having died four years earlier in his early fifties after battling pancreatic cancer.

During the next live dates, Marty was aware that he was being seen as something of a replacement for Jacka, especially as he now took lead vocal on some numbers that the latter used to sing. A few of these, such as 'Warm Feeling' and 'King's Cross Blues', were regarded as out of bounds and dropped from the set. The position he took on stage between Alan and Rod, he was well aware, was 'hallowed ground', but it had to be accepted that members did move on and leave groups. Nevertheless, he insisted that nobody could take Jacka's place, and he would never dream of trying to. One lady at the next Christmas shows at Newcastle City Hall after departure, who had been unaware that he was gone, demanded to know where he was and walked out in disgust.

Meanwhile, an ongoing project was about to bear fruit. Any group that had been going in various permutations for almost quarter of a century would inevitably have a vast backlog of unreleased material from studio demos, outtakes, radio sessions, and live recordings. The search was on as Ray and Dave Ian Hill, who had previously worked for the Virgin label and later became Lindisfarne's publicist as well as author of the first book about them, trawled through a mountain of reel-to-reel tapes, cassettes, and video recordings from their own archives. Material recorded by Lindisfarne, Brethren, Downtown Faction—admittedly a track or two from the Paul Jones Radio 2 1987 session, which someone had the foresight to tape from the radio, the original recordings having been wiped soon after broadcast—and Pacamax, the long-deleted Geordie Aid single 'Try Giving Everything', even a number from an old jam session by Rod with Mark Knopfler (taped at Rod's home in 1974) was all carefully sifted through. Selections were released on two CDs, *Buried Treasures Volumes One* and *Two*, in 1992. Once the hunt had begun, more and more inevitably came to light. There was soon enough for a third helping eight years later, and the possibility of even a fourth one day was not ruled out.

The year 1992 closed, not with a Christmas tour, which the group had decided would be dispensed with this time, but a single gig on 22 December at Newcastle City Hall. It was an opportunity to showcase new songs like Alan's 'Elvis Lives on the Moon' and Rod's 'Old Peculiar Feeling', and at the end of the first half a performance of 'Try Giving Everything', for which John Miles, writer Mike Waller, and several others came onstage to join in.

Early in the new year, the group returned to Hi-Level Studios. Results from the last recording session had proved unsatisfactory, and they decided 'another Gus Dudgeon' as producer was required. The task fell to Kenny Craddock, with whom they had not worked since the days of Lindisfarne Mk II. Since then, he had been musical director for acts such as Van Morrison, Paul Brady, and Gerry Rafferty. When asked, he was 'in a quandary about how best to approach it' as he knew everyone socially, but had not worked with them as a band for some time. In the best group tradition, he called a pub meeting, which gave everyone the chance to put forward any ideas and misgivings about the songs and arrangements. Everything was fully discussed before they entered the studio, and they all had a really good drinking session into the bargain. Naturally they were hardly in a fit state to begin working the next day, but when the time came to select songs for the new album, Steve Weltman also played a crucial role. Marty recalled that they wrote a load of material and Steve 'just tore them apart'. Only the very best got through.

Two numbers on what would become *Elvis Lives on the Moon* ended up as collaborations between Alan and Kenny. Despite the lack of a professional relationship for almost two decades, Kenny had long felt that they would reunite at some stage in the future. About two weeks after they returned from Russia, Alan called him up:

> He couldn't wait to tell me all about his experiences over there, he loved it—apart from the fact that he couldn't get a drink on the aeroplane!— and he said to me, 'I've written this lyric, but the tune I've got for it is crap.' So he sent me the lyric, this was 'Mother Russia' by the way, and I wrote a new tune for it, made a new demo of it with my vocal, sent it back within a couple of days and he loved it. Alan came down to my place and put his vocal on to a new demo and the collaboration went on from there, another new start in our ongoing friendship.[13]

After that, they promptly joined forces on two more, 'Demons' and 'Spoken Like a Man', a half-mournful, half-angry, slow-burning, and suddenly piercing, ramshackle blues and polished protest song all at once. With hindsight, the lyrics also had something of a farewell message from Alan as well.

'Old Peculiar Feeling', which had been a favourite on stage, seemed to lack something in the recorded version, until the group had another pub rendezvous to discuss the album's progress. Marty suggested they should try it more in the style of McGuinness Flint's 'When I'm Dead and Gone'. Rod had not been at the meeting, but after a phone call to his home, he reworked it, giving it a minor makeover with more prominent mandolin that provided the necessary ingredient. The group were thrilled with the result, Marty even thinking to himself that it was 'Meet Me on the Corner' all over again.[14]

To some extent *Elvis Lives on the Moon* was a concept album, revealing the inspiration of the group's tour of Russia and the poverty they had seen first-hand as one of the first Western acts to perform in the country before the iron curtain became history, with Alan's passionately political 'Mother Russia' and 'Day of the Jackal'. Closer to home was 'Soho Square', an indictment of inequality, with lyrics about 'pretty darlings everywhere dressed to kill from their heads to their feet' and the homeless who had had nothing past their lips for a week.

Once it was ready for release on their new label, Castle, the group went back on the road, playing festivals; they started with Torquay, Wath on

Dearne, and then Milton Keynes in April, followed by a week of shows in the United Arab Emirates. In June, there were three fleadhs in Glasgow, London, and Waterford respectively, where they shared billing with Van Morrison, Bob Dylan, The Pogues, Runrig, and John Martyn, and at the end of the month their first performance at Glastonbury in the acoustic tent alongside Sharon Shannon, The Blues Band, and Eddi Reader (formerly of chart-toppers Fairground Attraction). Glastonbury was 'brilliant', said Si: 'To see 3,000 people giving it "that" with their arms during 'Run for Home' was great'. Later that summer, there was another festival at Skagen, Denmark, where they played alongside Jack the Lad. The group had just reformed briefly to celebrate the reissue with bonus tracks of the three Charisma albums on CD, with a line-up consisting of Billy, Phil, and Walter, accompanied by Jed Grimes on guitar and Simon Ferry, who had played with Ian McCallum, on drums.

In August, there was another performance on the Newcastle Quay at the Tall Ships Festival, when they played on a stage designed as a masted ship. Joining them were Maxie and Mitch, The Doonans, Hedgehog Pie, and Jack the Lad, all the last three featuring the indefatigable Phil Murray in their line-up.

A subsequent date that month, at Newark Castle, was Si's farewell to the group, but an amicable one. He was about to fulfil the dream and an opportunity of a lifetime, an appropriate one for a former member of Lindisfarne—to settle in Toronto and begin a new career running his own brewery. For the last few months, he had been based in Canada, keeping his instruments in England so as to avoid additional flight costs for equipment while he commuted back and forth across the Atlantic to honour existing gigs. They stayed behind in England after he left the group, in case of possible future sorties. One interesting instrument followed him over the water: a Hamer electric, which he inherited after the death of his brother Marcus, a guitar roadie for one of Iron Maiden's guitarists.

On his departure, he said he had plenty of half-finished songs on tape that might end up on a solo album one day. Sadly, that was one dream that would remain unrealised during his remaining twenty years.

The temporary differences between Alan and Si during the early days had long since been forgotten. An older, wiser, and more forgiving Alan was not too proud to admit to the others that he had been way over the top with his criticisms. After Si left this time, he was 'quite choked' and would often remark on how much he missed his 'little pal'. Yet Si's *au revoir* eased the arrival of Kenny, the only one of the four recruits to Lindisfarne Mk II in 1973 who subsequently returned to the fold. He had been a natural choice after producing, playing on, and helping to write the album, and when they went on the road, he joined them on Hammond organ, piano, and guitar.

Elvis Lives on the Moon received little attention on release, a fate all too common to new product from groups of a certain vintage seen as appealing mainly to a niche, more mature market. Undaunted, the group undertook another tour in November and December with The Strawbs opening for them every night. It was an appropriate pairing as both groups, at their peak at around the same point in the early 1970s, had much in common. The Strawbs' frontman Dave Cousins, who readily praised Alan as an excellent songwriter, said that they too had never really regarded themselves as folk, but started in folk clubs as they played acoustic guitars and there was nowhere else to work. In Britain, there was something slightly derogatory about the folk-rock tag, and their reputation had also suffered from their highest charting single, in their case 'Part of the Union' in 1973, being more or less a novelty singalong and the only one for which everybody remembered them—even if they had at least not had a celebrity footballer on lead vocals.

The year 1994 opened with an acoustic tour by Alan and Kenny, playing accordion, keyboards, and acoustic slide, with singer-guitarist Miller Anderson, who had previously worked with the likes of Ian Hunter, T. Rex, and Mountain. It yielded *Another Little Adventure*, a live album taken from shows at the Blackheath Hall and Mean Fiddler, which gave Alan an opportunity to revisit old songs like 'Poor Old Ireland' and 'Winter Song' alongside 'Mother Russia' and 'Day of the Jackal', finishing up with a rousing 'Fog on the Tyne'.

Even prior to *Elvis Lives on the Moon*, Kenny had been collaborating with Alan on several songs, not only for the group, but also 'big ballad' style songs specifically written with other artists in mind. The one that might have had the most potential, 'Always It's You', had been intended for the Whitney Houston picture *The Bodyguard*. Kenny and Alan tried it out on several other people who said it was 'a fantastic song' and they got Lianne Carroll to sing on the demo:

'People were pitching from all over the place, because of the enormous amount of money involved,' said Kenny, 'there would be an almost guaranteed hit single, the film soundtrack itself, a soundtrack album and after they whittled all these songs down to a shortlist of about six, we were still in there! At the last minute, Kevin Costner said, "well I like this Dolly Parton song, I think this would be right," so they went with 'I Will Always Love You'. But Whitney had actually heard and liked our song.'[15]

In May and June, Rod Clements followed suit with his first solo tour and album. Once recognised purely as the fiddle and bass player of the group, who also embellished the songs in the studio with additional lead and slide guitar, he now fulfilled an ambition he had been nurturing for years, to play mainly acoustic and electric slide blues, with a combination of his own songs played his way. He had begun recording what was to develop into his solo debut, *One Track Mind*, two years earlier, at Redesdale Studios, Northumberland, with Geoff Heslop producing. As well as solo versions of 'Road to Kingdom Come' and 'Train in G Major', he also drew on old favourites like Dylan's 'Down in the Flood' and Woody Guthrie's 'Hard Travelling', intending to combine his own material with examples of the folk and blues tunes that had long inspired him. Critics praised the end result, likening his style to that of Ry Cooder. Rod's touring outfit comprised a trio, using Ray and Steve Cunningham as rhythm section, with one date also featuring Fraser Spiers on harmonica. When not playing on his own songs, he and Fraser played a few dates as part of Rab Noakes' new group The Varaflames.

In August, the group made a long-overdue debut at Fairport Convention's Cropredy Festival in Oxfordshire. Ray suggested with a smile that Dave Pegg, then playing bass guitar with Fairport, had been wanting them there for years, 'but he couldn't bear parting with the money!' Both contrasting, but quintessentially British acts had long been bracketed together ever since Brethren had been the support act for Fairport on several British college and club dates in the late 1960s, and they often appeared on the same bill at brewery-sponsored festivals. At Cropredy, their ninety minutes on stage to what might have been a more critical audience than most was proof, if any was needed, that they had developed into one of the finest roots-based groups of all.

Another compilation album, *Lindisfarne on Tap*, hit the shops around the same time. Castle had recently acquired the group's post-Charisma back catalogue and was keen to exploit it. The title was appropriate, given that the group were sponsored by Tap and Spile. A new single, 'We Can Make It', co-written by Alan and Ian McCallum, appeared simultaneously.

Later, in 1994, they went on tour again. Alan had returned from holiday with a severe throat infection and they needed to postpone a show at Ulverston, but his voice failed to improve over the next few shows, so they made some changes to arrangements in order to accommodate his severely limited vocal range. A few songs were dropped from the set and replaced with others that could be sung by Rod or Marty. The first few dates featured a solo set from Rod, and when Alan's voice improved, the solo spot was retained as it had gone down so well.

The tour was also notable for the introduction of another new member. Dave Denholm had been an art student at Newcastle College when he was initially contacted by Ray to help out. The connection had come about probably through Steve Daggett, who had produced a compilation album of tracks by local groups, including one by Dave's group This Is This. After becoming a roadie and guitar technician for the group, he played guitar while Rod contributed the mandolin part on 'Lady Eleanor'. By spring 1995, he was adding guitar and backing harmonies on nearly every song, and the obvious solution was for him to join full-time.

In March that year, they embarked on an overseas jaunt to venues where they had not played before, this time in the Middle East, at hotels and country clubs in Muscat, Abu Dhabi, Bahrain, and Qatar. Steve Cunningham was unable to join them as his wife was expecting a baby, so they recruited Ian Thomson on bass guitar. Ian had formerly been a member of Dust on the Needle, another local revolving doors outfit that had included Kathryn Tickell, members of Hedgehog Pie, and even Rod and Ray on occasion. One project followed another, as on their return home Rod went on tour as a soloist, supporting Robin Williamson from the Incredible String Band. Alan had his own plans for the spring, with a new solo studio album and nationwide tour. The musicians he had earmarked for the purpose were Dave Denholm on lead guitar, Frankie Gibbon on bass guitar, and Paul Smith on drums. The last two had already worked with him on *On the Other Side* some twelve years earlier.

As they say, where there's a hit there's a writ. In September 1994, Danish singer Whigfield made history by being the first act to enter the British singles chart at No. 1 (excluding Al Martino, who topped the first-ever chart in 1952) with her debut, 'Saturday Night', although sales well in excess of 1 million in Britain alone during the next year did not prevent *Smash Hits* readers from voting it the worst record of the year. Three months later, Alan was advised—strictly in the interests of research rather than self-entertainment—to take a close listen to the song. Hearing a few bars was enough to convince him that it was a blatant copy of 'Fog on the Tyne'. The tunes, he said, were similar and he counted eight notes in exactly the same place at exactly the same rhythm. 'At least ours was a good tune,' he commented, 'Whigfield's is just caterwauling over a repetitive drum beat.'[16] He considered taking it to court on a charge of plagiarism, but was deterred by the likely cost of such a case and was probably advised that it would be unlikely to succeed. Perhaps he had to agree with Keith Richards, who once observed that 'there's only one song in the world, and Adam and Eve wrote it'.[17]

The year 1995 was the group's twenty-fifth anniversary. On 10 June, BBC Radio 2 broadcast a one-hour documentary, *Meet Me on the Corner*. Produced by Rab Noakes, wearing his BBC hat as Robert Noakes, the outgoing head of musical entertainment of BBC Scotland; it featured extensive interviews with Ray, Rod, and Alan, and was presented by Tim

Healy. On 2 July 1970, Lindisfarne had played Newcastle City Hall for the first time as support act to Jackson Heights. The opportunity to play a special show to mark the occasion was too good to miss, and Tyne Tees planned to record it, with talk of a CD and video to follow afterwards. With Rab as support act, Lindisfarne put on an appropriately magnificent show, later released as promised under the title *Another Fine Mess*. They bookended the month on 28 July by headlining at the Cambridge Folk Festival, where, Paul Sexton reported for *The Times*, 'the new song 'Money' proved that the Geordies stand for more than mere nostalgia', but the singing along on the choruses of several of the old favourites 'carried way beyond the campsite'.[18]

In October, they played a week's tour, finishing at the Prince of Wales Centre in Cannock on the 22nd, at which Billy Mitchell came to see them. There was something rather prescient in hindsight about the occasion, for little did anyone know that it would be Alan's last gig with them.

During the next few weeks, he was working on a solo album with Dave supplying additional guitar. On 17 November, they were in the studio together, and both were very enthusiastic about how the sessions were turning out. The idea was to include new versions of several songs from his back catalogue, among them '100 Miles to Liverpool', 'This Heart of Mine', and 'Drug Song'. He remarked that it would sound 'autobiographical'.

That night he had a meal with Pat, and afterwards, he complained of severe chest pains. An ambulance was called, but by the time it arrived, he was dead from a massive heart attack. He was fifty years old.

'Alan had hit a really purple patch,' said Ray:

It began around *Amigos*—he seemed to find form again. I don't think people ever really appreciated him for the fine songwriter he was. He wrote some unique songs; they were northern in message. There's been nobody like him, very few people understood him as a writer or even came close to writing his way. His music should have delivered more for him than it ever did.[19]

In the House of Commons, David Clelland, MP for Tyne Bridge, sponsored an early day motion:

That this House notes with deep regret the sudden and tragic death of Alan Hull, leading member of the North East band Lindisfarne; notes that Alan not only brought great pleasure to millions of music lovers but was a dedicated socialist who cared deeply for his fellow man; extends deepest sympathy to Alan's wife Pat and their three daughters in their loss; and notes that their grief is shared by his many friends and colleagues and by Tyneside as a whole which has lost a great ambassador, a true Geordie and a good man.[20]

Taking their place alongside his widow (Pat), daughters (Rosamunde, Berenice, and Francesca), and granddaughter (Roxanne) at a humanist funeral in the chapel at North Shields Crematorium on 24 November, were Rod, Kenny Craddock, Marty, Dave, and Si, who had returned from Canada for the event. They performed three of his songs, 'One World' (the song written for Roxanne), 'Fog on the Tyne', and 'Alright on the Night'. Ray Laidlaw read a couple of poems from The Mocking Horse, and to finish with the assembled company sang John Lennon's 'Imagine', followed by 'Clear White Light'. Among those who had come to pay their respects were Jacka, Chris Rea, Brendan and Tim Healy, John Anthony, and Mickey Sweeney. Joe Mills, former regional chairman of the Labour Party, recalled for the benefit of the crowd that Alan had given faithful service to the cause, even to the extent of driving one year to the annual conference in Brighton so he could contribute to the Geordie night that was part of the delegates' social activities—and then drove straight back again. Mike Elliott delivered a eulogy recalling time spent in Alan's company, to much laughter. 'We're not here to be mournful,' he reminded them, 'There will be no dirges. If there are tears, let them be tears of joy.' As the curtain closed over the coffin, he said gently, 'Ta-ra, bonny lad.'[21]

Like the present members of the group, Jacka was shocked at his former colleague's untimely death, made all the sadder as they had never been reconciled and had not spoken to each other for years. 'There were lots of things that could have been said but weren't,' he said. He revealed much later that he had been talking to his Alan's widow, Pat, over the previous couple of years, and she said he was always very sorry for his attitude towards him at the end of his time with the group. He certainly wanted to make it up, but died before the chance arose: 'Alan was a very complex person underneath the persona. He was a great songwriter, very underrated and that probably got on his nerves'.[22]

For Ray, the situation was surreal, and for the first day or so after receiving the news, he could not believe Alan was gone:

I knew he wasn't well. He didn't look after himself. But Alan lived his life the way he liked to and he wouldn't have coped well with changing his diet or going to the gym. If someone had said to him when he was twenty-five you can live until you're fifty doing anything you want or live to seventy-five and make compromises, I know which one he would have picked.[23]

Minstrels for the North East

Would Lindisfarne survive the passing of their frontman, and did they ever have any doubts about continuing? As Ray said, it was 'the best way they could deal with his death'. Pat Hull gave them her full approval to open another chapter in the group's story. About three days after his passing, they got together at Rod's house in Rothbury, where 'there were lots of cups of tea and not knowing what to say'.[1] While they agreed unanimously that Alan was a huge part of the band, if they could find the right person to sing and play, they had to go on.

Fortunately, there was an obvious candidate to fill those huge boots. Billy Mitchell had been first in the frame some twenty-two years earlier when it seemed as if Alan was going to take a step back from live work, if not leave altogether, and they needed a replacement. In his heart, he said, he had always been part of the group, having 'celebrated their successes and shared their despair during difficult times'. Now he would play his part in helping them to keep the flame burning, as he had so nearly done once before.

Rod said that while Alan was irreplaceable, Billy's status as a performer and a friend qualified him uniquely for the task ahead. Ray was sure that it helped the grieving process, and that they 'got through losing Alan by continuing to perform his songs'. He was sure that nobody else could have slotted into the band as easily as Billy did. His former Jack the Lad colleague had a different approach to the man he was taking over from, but his interpretation of the material brought a new dimension to much of it and in the process, it invigorated their sound and performances. After roughly six months, he noted: 'It felt completely natural and he doubted very much that we could have achieved what we did in the eight years after Alan's passing without Billy's integrity and enthusiasm'.[2]

Rehearsals began in January 1996 for a postponed tour, rescheduled to begin in March. The next show at Hartlepool Town Hall was an emotional occasion. Several radio sessions were undertaken to promote the dates, and a decision was made to play shows in electric and acoustic formats, depending on the size of the venue. The first Untapped show was played on 18 May. Dave, Rod, and Marty shared the vocals with Ray using a three-piece drum kit and hi-hat sitting to their right. Billy was already committed to gigs as part of Maxie and Mitch in Canada, but with Lindisfarne having increasingly become a kind of extended family who could adapt themselves according to the personnel available, the arrangement worked well. A contributor to the group's fanzine remarked that the group was now a matter of 'no edge, no egos—just a collection of mates having a great time'. Split formats became as commonplace as regular rearrangements to the set, comprising many of the old favourites, newer songs, and tunes from the Woody Guthrie songbook, with 'Jackhammer Blues' making a regular reappearance.

Alan's presence was constantly with them. In June, his family and friends attended the scattering of his ashes at the mouth of the Tyne—and appropriately it turned out to be a foggy day. In the evening, they played a show in a marquee in the centre of Newcastle, another emotional affair, for the opening of Eurofest 96, to a crowd of 6,000. Back from Canada, Billy was now fully part of the group, as he announced with sadness that they 'said goodbye to a friend today'. The next generation was arriving, for augmenting the group were Marty's son, Andrew, and Billy's son, Tom. Two months later, Alan's last album *Statues and Liberties* was completed, and it released in November on the recently revived Transatlantic label, which had brought out his first solo single in 1969, to excellent reviews.

In December, as part of a twenty-nine-date British tour, the group recorded both nights of their *Untapped and Acoustic* performances at Marden High School, Tynemouth. The venue was appropriate as Dave Denholm had been there, as had Ray's son, Jed, and also Tom Mitchell. The record was initially available only by mail order and given a full release by Park Records, an independent label based in Oxford specialising in folk and roots music.

In early 1997, the group went to work at a new studio, Watercolour Music, Ardgour, Scotland. By now, they were without a producer, a problem they had never experienced in the past. Rod said it was very difficult for a group to produce itself, and the responsibility was that of Dave and himself much of the time on this occasion. The result was a four-track EP, *Blues from the Bothy*, including two of Rod's new songs, 'Coming Home to You' and 'Refugees'. The summer included several festival dates, and on August Bank Holiday weekend, they were present at the switching on of the Blackpool Illuminations. The event was broadcast live by Radio 2, with several BBC presenters, including Bob Harris, who announced them on stage.

Next was a thirty-three-date British tour from mid-October to the end of November, finishing on 29 November at Newcastle City Hall. The group were slightly nervous as it was the first time they had played there since the hallowed quarter-century concert with Alan, but by now they were so comfortable with the new line-up they need not have worried. Another first was scored on that occasion with the organisation of a fan convention, the highlight being a group-related photograph auction in aid of the North-East Young Musicians' Fund, promoted by Kathryn Tickell, their guest on stage that night.

In between tour dates, and radio sessions such as one for Radio 2's *Folk and Roots Show*, presented by Mike Harding, sessions continued for what would be the first album since the passing away of Alan. Rod had slipped with ease into the role of main songwriter. With modesty, he remarked that when Alan had the role, there was some frustration and possibly a little envy: 'But I had no business to be, because he was just more prolific and successful than I was'. Once they had had some time off, they would get together and play some new songs. He might produce a tape of two things he had sweated really hard over 'and [Alan] had about fifteen. And ten of them would be brilliant'.[3]

After over twenty years of being 'number two', Rod had been promoted. It was a situation comparable to that of George Harrison, once The Beatles had disbanded and he was free to use his compositions while recording *All Things Must Pass*. Some of Rod's songs were in the form of 'three-quarters-formed ideas', others rather less. Although several numbers from Lindisfarne's back catalogue had been entirely his own work, he felt the need of a collaborator, and found the right person in Nigel Stonier, who had already worked with him as producer for *Odd Man Out*. They ended up writing six songs together for what would be the next album, recorded over spring and summer 1998. Sid Griffin, guitarist with The Long Ryders and journalist, was invited to produce. As an American living in London, he saw himself as being 'an outsider' who had a completely different perspective from Geordies, and the culture of the drinking, scarf-waving, and Christmas shows. Nevertheless, he was well aware of the talent of Alan Hull and of the loss his death was to the world, and as he was now gone, '[they had] to make do with what tools [were] at hand'.[4]

The record was something of a family affair—in that Billy Mitchell's other son, Scott, played piano on one song, 'Ghost in Blue Suede Shoes'. Moreover, Dave was now Dave Hull-Denholm, having just married Alan's daughter, Francesca, in a simple ceremony, with the group unaware until after the occasion. As Pat said, Alan had looked on Dave as the son he never had.

Here Comes the Neighbourhood was released in the summer. It was very much a group album, and although Rod's presence as songwriter was felt heavily, Billy and Marty each contributed one number. It was generally agreed that the yearning love song 'Can't Do Right for Doing Wrong', one of Rod's collaborations with Nigel Stonier, was the record's outstanding number. Five years later, it became a hit. It had been taken up by Ian Brown, who at the time was managing Nigel's wife, Thea Gilmore, in order to pitch it around his contacts and he asked sixteen-year-old Erin Rocha to demo it for him. He had been looking for more of a name to record it, but Eddy Grant, no stranger to the charts himself over the years as guitarist with The Equals and then as a soloist, was so impressed that he advised Ian to 'get the song out there' regardless of the artist. Erin's version was therefore developed and released, and the result was a Top 40 single over Christmas 2003.

Songwriting, Billy admitted, was never his strong suit. He had co-written a few numbers while he was with The Callies and with Jack the Lad, but on the whole, he was content to leave it to others—a matter of 'if Alan Hull can do it, let's give it a go'. It was not as easy for them as they thought:

Hully had a gift, we tried quite hard. I still have to try hard, songwriting doesn't come naturally to me, it's a blank sheet of paper and a lot of work. I always need pushing to write stuff, a commission with a definite subject, and a deadline, is always a help.[5]

Rod was delighted with the album, perhaps even more proud of it than any previous one he had been associated with. To him it was certainly up to the standard of *Nicely out of Tune* and *Fog on the Tyne*. Much of this was down to the collective feel, being less centred on one person's songs, one person's voice or set way of playing. All of them found Sid a pleasure to work with as producer. When they were planning the *Neighbourhood* album, they wanted somebody aware of their history, but someone who could help them to move on without losing out on the essence of the group. Ray put his name forward as they had met a couple of times earlier because he was an old pal of Ian Thomson's and they had been in bands together in the States. Unfortunately, Ray injured his back shortly before they had planned to start recording, and as with their limited budget, they needed to make the most of their studio time, so Sid and the others put all the tracks down with a click track, allowing Ray to overdub the drums once he was fit again.

As it had been their first studio album without Alan, they were a little nervous about how it would be received. Ray looked on it as something of a milestone in their history, as the very first one to feature Rod as the main writer and Billy as the main singer.

In the summer of 1999, they returned to America for a twenty-date tour. Quite apart from personnel changes, it was in many ways a very different Lindisfarne from the temporarily dispirited unit who had found it such an unwelcome slog twenty-seven years earlier. The American media were at something of a loss as to how to label their music. 'How do I answer that?' asked Ian Thomson, 'It's song-based; it's just the way it comes out.' Rod elaborated on what was a pretty all-embracing blend, saying that over many years, they had presented the songs in any way they could with the tools of rock and roots-type music:

> It's whatever we've been exposed to: Celtic, pop, folk, dance. We worked
> it into being, for some time, completely acoustic. Back then, it was
> something completely new and refreshing, and it was successful.[6]

A reviewer of one gig in June at the Berger Performing Arts Center, Arizona, commented that Celtic, rock, bluegrass, and country could all be heard 'in the band's tailored twenty-one-song set'. It was a set consisting largely of material drawn from *Here Comes the Neighbourhood* and choice back-catalogue items and drew warm praise, with an honourable mention for Billy as lead vocalist, 'comfy on stage as a night of must-see TV in his T-shirt and baggy pants (sans socks and shoes), [who] bounded about the stage and sang like a man twenty years younger'. 'Old Peculiar Feeling' and 'Two Way Street' were introduced by Billy as a pair of songs ideal for line dancing. 'Anyone caught line dancing will be immediately thrown out,' he quipped.[7] As had been the case on many an occasion at a show back in England, anybody who had still been sitting down throughout the rest of the set was soon up on their feet for 'We Can Swing Together'.

During the tour, Si crossed the border to meet up again and join them on stage during 'Uncle Sam' and 'Fog on the Tyne'. A friend of his, Graham Freed, another ex-pat from his Toronto local, The Feathers, flew him and a couple of mates in his four-seater 1973 Aerostar mid-wing twin-engined aircraft to see the group in Cincinnati. What happened next at that joyous reunion is best related in Si's inimitable style:

> The Ohio customs guys were putting in overtime at the weekend to meet
> us and gave one of our crew, Brian, a hard time determining whether or
> not the cigar he had brought from Canada was of Cuban origin (Nobody
> could work it out so they let us in). Graham parked the plane and we got a
> cab downtown and visited a couple of fantastic brewpubs before meeting
> the lads at the private garden party—which was the gig. Had a complete

blast of a night and got up at the end for a couple of tunes. Enjoyed myself so much that as I was strumming along I hardly noticed Mitch mouthing at me during 'Fog on the Tyne': 'Si. Hello. Earth to Si. It's your verse now. Remember?' We ran out of beer near the end of the evening (Americans unprepared for Geordies) so we had a whip round and I was directed to a gem of a local off licence and came back with some of the best beers in the US, which in this day and age of brewing, means the world. It seems I'm still the band's part time beer monitor, too, in my spare time.[8]

This American trip was so successful that they went back a second time the following summer. By then, another change in the line-up had come with Marty's departure for a new trio, The Happy Cats. It was closely followed by Rod's solo album *Stamping Ground*, and an outing on CD of his previous cassette-only album, *One Track Mind*.

In the winter of 2001, they gathered at Chapel Studios, Lincolnshire, to record what would almost certainly be the last new album under the name of Lindisfarne, with Nigel Stonier in the producer's chair. Completed and released in the spring of 2002, *Promenade* was an excellent swan song and a fresh milestone in Rod's own personal development as a singer-songwriter. Only one song, 'Freedom Square', written after watching the first episode of Ken Burns' TV series *Jazz*, was penned by him alone, but his status as the group's principal songwriter at this time was not up for negotiation, as he was involved as co-writer on a further nine out of thirteen. Of these, five songs were credited to Rod and Nigel, and three ('Coming Good', 'Candlelight', and 'Remember Tomorrow') were the work of a trio comprising Rod, Nigel, and Dave Hull-Denholm. That left 'Rock 'n' Roll Phone', the work of Billy, Rod and Nigel. This time Rod took lead vocals on both 'Freedom Square' and 'Significant Other'. The only previous occasion on which he had sung lead on a track in the studio was on the third verse of 'Knacker's Yard Blues' on the B-side of the first single in 1970.

Billy contributed a particularly moving number on the subject of family and old age, 'Happy Birthday Dad'. He summed up the bittersweet theme of the lyric as one of an ageing father seeming happy enough in a care home, perhaps because he had forgotten how to remember to be sad and what was he sad about anyway. He could not quite remember in the first place, but he thought he would be going home soon, even though he was well looked after where he was, with visitors always welcome, even if they did not come very often—who could blame them as he did not know who they were half the time. It was a sad scenario, but one with which many a middle-aged person with an elderly parent suffering from Alzheimer's disease could readily identify.

After the album was completed, they streamlined temporarily that summer as Lindisfarne Acoustic, a trio consisting of Dave, Rod, and Billy, and they released a live acoustic CD in time for their American tour.

The summer was marred by sad and unexpected news. During the previous year, Kenny Craddock and his partner, Julia, had settled in Portugal where he was going to build his own studio. In May 2002, soon after completing a solo album, his first, *Mad as the Mist and Snow*, he was killed in a car crash in the Algarve, aged fifty-two.

Another repercussion came from the past in 2003. By this time, Jacka had put his musical career on one side to revisit his original love of art. He had just opened a gallery in Witney, Oxfordshire, where he sold his paintings, specialising in painting buses and other vehicles in local settings, as well as accepting commissions for house portraiture and favourite buildings. About eight years earlier, his solo on 'Maggie May' was used in a bank commercial, making Rod Stewart and his co-writer Martin Quittenton an estimated £50,000 each in additional royalties. Believing that Jacka was entitled to a proportion of this sum, Barry McKay contacted Rod Stewart's legal representatives but without success.

There the matter might have ended. It was reopened after a similar legal case arose when Bobby Valentino, a session violinist who had contributed to the Bluebells' 'Young at Heart', a Top 10 hit first time around in 1984 and a No. 1 on reissue after being used in a Volkswagen television commercial in 1993 (and received a session fee of £75), took The Bluebells to court for unpaid royalties in respect of his contribution. He was awarded damages of £100,000 after the judge ruled in his favour. Claiming that he might have lost up to £1,000,000 through not being credited as a co-writer of 'Maggie May', Jacka said in a statement that he was convinced that his contribution to the record, which occurred in the early stages of his career just as he was just becoming famous for his work with Lindisfarne, was essential its success. Furthermore, a writing credit would have given him a professional status, which would have encouraged his writing efforts and could well have opened further doors for him. A spokesman for Rod Stewart described the claim as 'ridiculous', saying it was accepted that Mr Jackson played on the song, but not that he had any part in writing it: 'As is always the case in the studio, any musical contributions he may have made were fully paid for at the time as "work-for-hire"'.

The case never came to court. 'You have to let it go,' he said resignedly, 'I am proud of the work I did.'[9]

In August 2003, Lindisfarne played a well-received set at Cropredy, lasting two hours. Jacka was among those in the audience, and he watched them with mixed feelings. While acknowledging that it was a good performance, he did not really feel that he wanted to be up there on stage with them.

'Group members have come and gone over the years,' Ray once said, 'but belonging to Lindisfarne became more than just playing in a band, it was a way of life. We were equally at home in stadiums or in the back of pubs and clubs because the music came across whatever the venue.'[10]

Yet the way of life was soon to be no more. During the 2003 autumn tour, it was announced that Lindisfarne would shortly go their separate ways. After a chequered history extending back over thirty years, admittedly with the occasional break, it was coming to the finishing line. According to a reviewer who caught one of their final shows, they believed it was time 'to call an orderly and tidy end to a fantastically rewarding chapter of their lives'.[11]

The full picture was a little more complex than that. After Alan's death, his replacement with Billy and the departure of Steve Weltman as their manager, Ray had completely taken over managerial duties so everything to do with the group was in-house. During the last few years, they found it increasingly difficult to achieve an enthusiastic consensus on a number of issues, such as touring policy, promotion of new albums, and how to incorporate newer songs from the final two albums into the set. After a time, it was clear there were two camps in the band, with Billy and Ray in one, Rod, Dave, and Ian in the other. When things came to a head during the 2003 autumn tour, they decided to pack it in after the last date. Rod believed that they probably should have done it sooner: 'It actually came as a bit of a relief and I was glad of the opportunity to pursue my solo direction'.[12]

Their final gig as a full group was played at a packed Newcastle Opera House on 1 November, captured on DVD, video, and CD as *Time Gentlemen Please*. After the group came on stage and Billy announced sadly to the audience that it was the worst day of his life—'Alan Shearer [the Newcastle United striker] missed a penalty!'—they stormed into a powerful set, with an interval halfway through. The set included songs from the older albums and the more recent, as well as 'Rocking Chair', which he introduced as a song by Jack the Lad who 'filled in for Lindisfarne last time they split up'. Further on in the show, he quipped that he had split up from his wife, Lorraine, on a Tuesday, but on the following Friday, he had started going out with Clara the barmaid—'I Can See Clara Now Lorraine Has Gone'. Dave paid a touching tribute to his father-in-law with 'Winter Song' and 'January Song', and close to the end of the set, a rousing 'Run for Home' brought a tear to many an eye as the audience clapped, waved, and sang along until they were completely hoarse. Six days later, Tyne Tees TV showed a programme, *Northstars—Run for Home* on 7 November 2003, which told the story of the band, including footage of the final Opera House concert. However, a press campaign to award the status of Freemen of Newcastle to each member of the group came to nothing.

For the next few months, the spirit of the group continued on the live circuit. Lindisfarne Acoustic, a trio comprising Rod, Billy, and Dave, honoured remaining commitments and continued to tour until a last gig on 17 May 2004, the closing date of the 'Final Fling Tour', at the Elgiva Theatre, Chesham.

Afterwards, they could all look back with satisfaction on how the group had lasted, not least in dealing with the major shock of Alan's death. Ray spoke for them all when he said he did not have any preconceptions as to how long they would have stayed together after November 1995. At first, he had been unsure as to how the fans would react to Lindisfarne without Alan. Some, he anticipated, 'couldn't cope with it and to them Lindisfarne was over', while others had been prepared to give them a fair chance. Fortunately for the group, they were impressed with what they heard and that gave them the confidence they needed to continue:

> I'm glad we did, we made some great music and had lots more adventures but it certainly didn't feel like eight years, it passed by in a flash and now it's history. As my old Gran used to say, "memories are better than dreams"'.[13]

The flame was kept alight further when Rod, Dave, and Ian continued to play together as The Ghosts of Electricity, taking their name from a line in Bob Dylan's 'Visions of Johanna', with Rod doing a few solo gigs as well. Later that year, they played a show at Market Bosworth Rugby Club, which lasted for nearly two hours. It was an ideal showcase for several of Rod's solo numbers, including the poignant 'Cowboy in the Rain', a song about the tragic story of the late ex-Byrds member Gene Clark, who had famously drunk his dressing room dry while on tour with Lindisfarne, and 'When Jones Comes To Town', alongside 'Can't do Right for Doing Wrong' (fresh from its appearance in the Top 40 thanks to Erin Rocha) and inevitably 'Meet Me on the Corner'. Highlights were released on the album *Live Ghosts*, and reviewers were unstinting in their praise. One summed up the views of many in a pithy 'Lindisfarne are dead—long live Lindisfarne!' while the American journal *Sing Out!* proclaimed 'John Sebastian meets Ry Cooder meets Richard Thompson'. In 2006, they became a quartet with the addition of drummer Paul Burgess, the same year that Rod released another album, *Odd Man Out*.

In addition, he was one of several highly acclaimed folk and roots musicians enlisted to perform on a one-off charity single by Folk for

Peace, his contribution consisting of dobro and backing vocals. The song, 'Rumours of Rain', was written by Cathryn Craig and Brian Willoughby, and also included Martin Carthy, Ralph McTell, Tom Paxton, Nanci Griffith, Benny Gallagher, Clive Gregson, Jacqui McShee, Rick Kemp, and various present and past members of Fairport Convention. Rod had met Brian some years previously when The Strawbs were on tour with Lindisfarne, and they had renewed their acquaintance when setting up a Cathryn & Brian gig at Rothbury Roots in October 2003. His contribution was scheduled to be recorded in early April, when a break in Lindisfarne Acoustic's Final Fling tour coincided with one of Cathryn & Brian's visits to the North East; all he had to do was find a local studio willing to give them half a day, turn up, and sing a couple of lines over the work-in-progress that the duo would bring with them. A demo CD of the song and a lyric sheet duly arrived and accompanied him for the first part of the tour, to be practised to in quiet moments. The record was released on 29 November on the Hypertension label.

Though he continued to make occasional appearances on drums, Ray spent much of his time pursuing a new career in film and media production, generally co-producing with Geoff Wonfor. Geoff's involvement with Lindisfarne had dated back to his early years as a director of music films for the BBC, including a video of the group 'in suits with dickie bows', performing 'Run for Home' on a rooftop overlooking St James' Park, and his stock had risen through his involvement with The Beatles as director of their *Anthology* series. Between them, they were responsible for several show-business-related documentaries and DVDs of concerts, notably one of Jools Holland and Friends live at the Royal Albert Hall, a concert in aid of the Teenage Cancer Trust, as well as on various natural history subjects.

Over the next few years, most of the Lindisfarne family were heavily involved in working for charities and good causes. One of the most important projects was *Sunday for Sammy*, a biannual charity concert in aid of the Sammy Johnson Memorial Fund, staged at Newcastle, which became a regular event in 2004. Gateshead-born Sammy Johnson, once an aspiring guitarist, had turned to acting with leading roles in television's *Auf Wiedersehen, Pet* and *Spender*, then became a scriptwriter and moved to Spain where he died suddenly in 1998, aged forty-nine. After his death, the fund was established from an idea by Tim Healy, Jimmy Nail, and friends of Sammy to raise funds for young performing artists in the North East. Musical items and comic sketches always made up the programme, with several Lindisfarne members performing their songs, alongside occasional appearances from other local artists like Brian Johnson and Mark Knopfler. There was a thin line between the two, as Jacka was to be seen leading the audience in a heartfelt chorus at the end of 'Run for

Home' and also taking part in one of the *Auf Wiedersehen, Pet* sketches. Billy and Brian also once memorably took centre-stage together, bringing the house down with the traditional 'Geordie's Lost His Liggie'.

At other times of the year, Billy toured with Brendan Healy as part of the music and comedy double act Bill and Bren, playing with The Billy Mitchell Band that his son, Tom, and Ray Laidlaw, and making an appearance at the Cropredy Festival. With his background in comedy, it was only natural for him to appear in pantomime at Christmas, one year as an ugly sister in Cinderella, another as Igor the Useless in Babes in the Wood, and as part of Maxie & Mitch in Sleeping Beauty, portraying the royal bodyguards Hank and Marvin. Steve Daggett also headed a charity initiative as annual co-organiser basis of the Heroes and Scarecrows gigs, held from 2004 onwards at the Magnesia Bank public house in aid of the BBC's Children in Need campaign, with Si Cowe returning from Canada especially for the occasion, and Ian Thomson and Dave Hull-Denholm also taking part. Billed on local radio as 'a musical evening celebrating the songs and life of Alan Hull', it included an auction of Lindisfarne and Alan Hull memorabilia. Assorted personnel and songs from their back catalogue were often to be seen and heard on local stages, such as a concert in aid of the Teenage Cancer Trust at The Sage, Gateshead, in September 2006. Among the highlights was a group comprising Billy Mitchell, Jools Holland, Alan Clark of Dire Straits, and others backing Paul Weller on 'Meet Me on the Corner'.

On 19 November 2005, ten years after Alan's passing, friends and colleagues staged a celebratory gig in aid of the North East Young Musicians Fund at Newcastle City Hall. Among them were many Lindisfarne members past and present alongside Mike Elliott, Alan Clark, Frank Gibbon, Brendan and Tim Healy, Ian McCallum, Jimmy Nail, Tom Pickard, Kathryn Tickell, and Prelude. An interview with Alan and clips from the 1975 BBC2 play *Squire* were shown on a big stage screen. Guest artistes, most of whom had some Alan connection, played cover versions of his songs to an eager audience. Si Cowe and Ian McCallum both crossed the Atlantic to be there, and Jacka came out of his self-imposed musical retirement. The Motorettes, including Ray's sons, Jack and Jed, caused a minor sensation among the audience by performing a grunge version of 'I Hate to See You Cry'. Terry Morgan provided a monologue and Tom Pickard gave a reading from Alan's *The Mocking Horse*. Proceeds from the concert, filmed and released on DVD, were donated to The North East Young Musicians Fund, and the Alan Hull Award for young musicians in the North East was set up a year later in response to the success of the concert.

Jacka had evidently got the performing bug again. It was the first time in fifteen years that he had stepped out on to the stage at Newcastle

City Hall. Since 1990, he had put music on the back burner apart from occasional informal performances for friends. Having had his fill of touring, which had increasingly become an expensive chore, especially after the hits dried up, he was insistent that he would only return to live work at a certain level, and would never to go back to playing smoky bar rooms any more. However, The Gathering promised to be something different—a folk super group in which he was joined by Jerry Donahue (formerly Fairport Convention and Fotheringay guitarist), his daughter, Kristina, Rick Kemp, Doug Morter (formerly guitarist with Hunter Muskett), the Albion Band and Magna Carta, and Clive Bunker (former Jethro Tull drummer). The idea had originated with Jerry and agent Peter Barton asking old friends if they would participate on an occasional basis.

Originally billing themselves as The Gathering of Legends of Folk Rock, the name was soon shortened to The Gathering as rehearsals began in the summer of 2007 and they began playing live towards the end of the year in Britain, Germany, and the USA (where they were known as Gathering Britannia), fitting in gigs between their other groups, or in Jacka's case, when not painting or running the art gallery. Punters who saw the group were treated to see him fronting the group on 'Lady Eleanor', not only playing mandolin, but also singing lead. Two other songs that featured regularly in their set from the Lindisfarne songbook were 'This Has Got to End' and 'Kings Cross Blues', which he could comfortably play once again now that a suitable amount of time had elapsed since the station disaster. Due to what they called 'economics of the road' and other member commitments, it later slimmed down to a trio of Jerry, Doug, and Jacka, renamed Acoustic Gathering.

In 2006, Dave Hull-Denholm and poet Paul Summers recorded a CD, *Home in 3 Bits*, with Rod on dobro, Ian Thomson on bass, and cellists Greg Pullen and Cathy Donnelly. It was sold as 'essentially a phantom soundtrack for a never-to-be-made short film' and 'an innovative and imaginative poetic travelogue set to music inspired by the Northumberland coast'.

As the group's main songwriter and solo artist, it was only to be expected that Rod's solo career would flourish. In 2008, there was a second reissue of his 1994 debut solo album *One Track Mind*, with two bonus tracks added, 'A Dream Within a Dream' and 'Blues for a Dying Season'. Both songs went back to the start of his career, the former having been performed on an early Lindisfarne radio broadcast and the latter recorded by Downtown Faction, but as-yet unreleased in any form. Both versions of 'No Turning Back' were included, the studio version not having been available on CD before.

Six years later, he released a twenty-six-track double album. Having long thought about assembling his lyrical back catalogue anew, in November 2012, he began regular recording sessions in Ron Angus' Chester-le-Street studio. The result was *Rendezvous Café*, featuring stripped-back solo versions of his own compositions originally recorded by the group, and in a couple of cases by other people as well, among them 'The Road to Kingdom Come', 'Don't Ask Me', 'Unmarked Car', 'Can't do Right for Doing Wrong', and, naturally, 'Meet Me on the Corner'. For him it was the fulfilment of a personal ambition: 'It feels like a body of work and I'm proud of it…. It's nice to have been able to gather these songs together in one place and let people know that I wrote them'. The front cover of the CD was designed by Lindisfarne's last bassist Ian Thomson who played live and recorded with Rod. Ian played with him at the launch of the album, held in the Tyneside Cinema's Classic screen in April 2014.

Sometimes, there was no substitute for a songwriter's own versions of his material. 'The main thing is that it's my voice—the writer speaks if you like—so it's not Jacka or Billy or Dave Hull-Denholm,' he said:

> Although they all did great jobs, I've always had this belief that the writer can sing it like nobody else can—not as well maybe—but they bring something to it which no one else could. I've always maintained that a good song would stand up on its own two legs whoever is doing it. This is me kind of putting my money where my mouth is I suppose.[14]

He was confident that people wanted to hear them, as whenever he had been playing his own gigs as a soloist or with other musicians, people would ask him afterwards whether he had a CD containing his own versions, and until then he always had to say no. The nostalgia of putting the collection together had been enjoyable, though he was eager to get back to the creative process of making new music afterwards:

> Some of the songs I hadn't revisited for a long time so it was nice to remember where they came from and bring them back to life. But I also feel in a way the album is drawing a line under what has been done. I'm letting everybody know that these are all my songs and they're all here in one place for the first time, stripped down to as basic form as you can get really. Now I can move onto some new stuff. For me, songwriting has always been as the mood takes me.[15]

Much of the older and long unavailable music from the Lindisfarne family was reappearing on CD. A tenth-anniversary compilation of Alan's work, beginning with the two Chosen Few singles and his early debut on the

Transatlantic label and ending with the last group and solo studio and live albums released before his death, found a berth on the *We Can Swing Together* anthology on Castle in 2005. A few years later, *Phantoms*, supplemented by material from Radiator's *Isn't It Strange* (the rights of which had reverted to Alan's widow, Pat), were issued on the Market Square label; in addition, the almost-forgotten *Happy Daze* album (with bonus tracks in the form of early demos recorded by Alan in 1969), a solo concert by Alan at Clifton Polytechnic in November 1975 (*Alright On The Night*), and Jack the Lad's final set *Jackpot* (again with additional studio and live recordings seeing the light of day for the first time) were released. EMI, which had acquired the Virgin catalogue, issued a four-disc set *The Charisma Years* in 2011, welcomed particularly for a few alternative mixes and some material appearing for the first time. Like other albums of their era, they had sometimes gone out of critical favour, but were now ripe for re-evaluation by the more discerning. The BBC archives also provided rich pickings for further albums from the group and from Alan as a soloist.

Although Alan was gone, he was still fondly remembered in his native Newcastle. Barry McKay had long been at the forefront of a public move for a memorial plaque on the front of the City Hall, scene of so many of the group's triumphs on stage. It was endorsed by several figures from the musical and political world. Among them were Lord Kinnock, who said that there needed to be a permanent, visible memorial to Alan in his home city as in his work and his life he had been such an inspiration to countless people who shared his convictions of freedom and justice:

> His music delighted, it intrigued, it was always full of humanitarian purpose and it had a marvellous mixture of gravity and humour. Above all, his democratic socialist commitment to peace and to opportunity, care and security for people of all ages, both sexes and every creed and ethnic background should be highlighted as practical ideals that have enduring value for all generations.

Another fervent supporter was Dennis Skinner, MP for Bolsover, who called him 'a true working class champion who never forgot his roots and was always there for the workers when they were engaged in battle [who] lived a true socialist life'.[16]

The Newcastle City Council plaque, honouring the memory of Alan and the group outside the City Hall for his contribution towards helping bring the city and the north east area into focus, was unveiled on 19 July 2012. Hundreds of fans attended the ceremony, and after the unveiling a trio comprising Jacka, Dave and Ian played a short set of Alan's songs outside in the open air. Alan's daughter Rosamunde said that the family was particularly touched and proud, knowing that her father, who had been so proud of his Geordie roots, would be honoured to have his name outside a venue so closely associated with him. Jacka quipped that he had been looking forward to the day, and 'to performing in the street outside the City Hall instead of inside it for a change'. For him, it was a further link with the past which he once thought he had put behind him. He had never played with Ian or Dave before the plaque unveiling, but he could not believe Dave's voice and how similar he sounded to Alan. 'When me and him sing together I sometimes have to look over my shoulder, it's eerie.'[17]

The group's presence was also kept alive by the birth of another new project, the Lindisfarne Story. Devised and presented by Billy and Ray, it had started with them talking about it in the pub one evening, and then busking it at the Customs House Theatre in South Shields twenty-four hours later, telling stories about the group and performing an unplugged selection of the songs. It went down so well that they developed it into a full show in its own right, playing smaller venues as a duo and larger venues with video clips and photographs on-screen, aided and abetted by a six-piece Lindisfarne Band, who recreated the original sound on stage with a performance including the complete *Fog on the Tyne* album in sequence. As Ray explained: 'When you break it down, Lindisfarne's criteria was always the song; whether the songs worked with one person or the full band. Now we're stripping them down to almost nothing, they can work again with just the two of us, just as they can work with six'.[18]

Ironically in November 2012, less than five months after Alan's plaque was unveiled, the city council announced that as part of a cost-cutting process the future of the City Hall was under review, with a possibility of the venue being closed or handed over to an external operator. Jacka was foremost among those incensed that 'councillors, magistrates, men of renown' had such disregard for the building and its place in rock culture as their premier music venue. It was of particular significance to him and the group since they had played there over 120 times in their career over three decades.

Yet this cloud had a silver lining, for the result was to be the return of the group after more than nine years. A petition with 13,000 signatures protesting against closure was presented to the council on 31 January 2013 by members of the Facebook North East Music History Group. After talking to Barry McKay, Jacka announced that the newly convened Ray Jackson's Lindisfarne would return there in December for a revival of the Christmas shows to demonstrate their support for keeping the doors open, in what would be his first performance there in twenty-three years. Tickets sold out in a mere six hours, much to Jacka's surprise as it had been over twenty years since he left: 'Over that time I had expected the memory of my contribution to it to have dimmed'. To him, the demand was proof that there was 'still a flame burning in peoples' hearts to hear the songs sung and played once more by an original front man and at their favourite venue'.[19] Second and third shows were added, tickets were likewise snapped up almost at once, and extra dates were added at Middlesbrough, Harrogate, and Hull.

Ray Jackson's Lindisfarne was a reversion to the six-piece format, which now also included Dave Hull-Denholm, Charlie Harcourt, Ian Thomson, and Steve Daggett. Jacka said he needed to have Dave and Ian in the line-up as the feedback from everyone who saw them play together at the plaque unveiling had been exceptionally positive. The new drummer, another Tyneside musical veteran, was Paul Thompson, formerly of Roxy Music and Bryan Ferry's band on record and tour for much of his career as a soloist.

That autumn, as the time drew nearer, Jacka was asked—tongue-in-cheek, one assumes—whether Gazza would be appearing on stage with him. Jacka conceded that Gazza, whom he had never met, was 'a very funny and entertaining guy', much loved in the area, a great footballer, and a Geordie hero, but no musician, while he, Ray Jackson, could never play football. Looking back on the infamous 'Fog on the Tyne (Revisited)', he recognised that the single had reached No. 2 and that the rest of the group 'therefore achieved what they had set out to do', but that the good name of Lindisfarne had suffered as a result. He drew a parallel with Jeff Beck, who had never wanted to record 'Hi Ho Silver Lining', but was pressured into it by producer Mickie Most who knew it would be a smash, and even though it continued to be a much played record over the years, 'it feels like wearing a pink toilet seat round your neck for the rest of your life'.[20]

The shows in December 2013 were inevitably a great success. As in the old festive concerts more than thirty years before, they started with the front of house asking punters as they came through the doors to select a party hat in exchange for their tickets, as they took their seats to the sound of Christmas carols on the City Hall pipe organ. A Geordie Santa introduced the group before they took to the stage with a lengthy show in which the favourites came thick and fast in two sets, separated by a short interval. For encores, there were 'Let's Stick Together', a nod to Paul Thompson's stint as Bryan Ferry's drummer, and an uplifting version of 'Clear White Light'.

There were more shows in 2014, including three at Newcastle in the week before Christmas and additional dates at Middlesbrough and Hull. Jacka was in his element as ever with his off-the-cuff spoken introductions to each song and quips to the audience. They were really good, he told them after one particularly hearty singalong, asking with a wink whether they had been on the brown ale. At the beginning and end of 'Court in the Act', he played the intro from 'Maggie May' and said afterwards that it was on a record by somebody whose name slipped his mind. 'I actually did get recognition at long last,' he added to much laughter and applause, in a sly reference to Rod Stewart's recent memoirs: 'It was in his autobiography—I bought it in Oxfam the other week just to make sure I was in!'

To quote the title of another of Rod's songs on which Jacka had played mandolin in 1974, it would be 'Farewell' after that. In January 2015, he issued a statement thanking fans for their support and good wishes during the last two seasons of gigs as he stepped down. For years he had been turning down the chance to work again in a new line-up, and had only got involved again because of the campaign to help save the City Hall from closure. That had been achieved, and since listening to and taking notice of objectors who wrote in and signed the petition in their thousands, the City Council had committed sufficient funding to keep the Hall from closing. For the time being at least, its future was secure.

In the process, he had enjoyed two consecutive years of practically sell-out shows. He had thoroughly loved performing songs again, which the original group had recorded in the 1970s, and he was very glad that the fans had a chance to relive the experience with him one more time. It had never been a long-term plan and he wished the others all the best in the future. A posting on the 'Lindisfarne Official' Facebook page from the rest of the group said that although his decision had come as a surprise to them, it was always his intention 'to hand things over at some point and ensure the great name of Lindisfarne continues to keep the songs and spirit alive well into the future'.

Back came their former bass guitarist and violinist, thereafter one of their guitarists and vocalists, to take up the baton as the frontman of Rod Clements's Lindisfarne. Following the announcement, he posted on Facebook to thank fans for their positive comments. Jacka's decision to retire marked the end of an era, he agreed, but the group had 'never been about any one individual' and he was keen to assure everybody who cared about their history and future that the rich legacy of music, songs, and live performances associated with the name could not be in safer hands. The reconstituted line-up was a highly accomplished bunch of musicians, most of whom he had known for years, bound together by mutual respect and a shared enthusiasm for the best of what the group had achieved over the years. Dave added that they could now look forward to taking their unique sound back on the road in earnest, as they reasserted Lindisfarne's place as one of British music's great live acts and continued to ensure that Alan Hull's rich musical legacy would live on.

The six-piece group expanded on occasion to a seven-piece with the addition of Tom Leary, from Feast of Fiddlers, on fiddle and additional vocals. From then on, it was business as usual, with a full schedule of gigs at venues and festivals throughout Britain.

That autumn was overshadowed by another passing in the Lindisfarne family. In Toronto, Si had become ill with cancer of the oesophagus, and on 30 September, he died in his sleep, aged sixty-seven. His old colleagues were quick to pay tribute to their colleague who had been an integral member for the best part of twenty years. Ray Laidlaw said in a local radio interview that he had made an immense contribution as an exquisite musician, very off-the-wall, who never took the easy option:

> [He never did] the predictable stuff … in the early days a lot of the quirkiness came from Lindisfarne: those guitar tunings, the sweet and sour harmonies—he was the one behind that, lots of strange instrumentation and arranging. It was a large part of what made the band different and special.

Jacka recalled with affection 'the special relationship formed by the five of [them] in [their] two periods together, totalling twenty years [that] cannot be underestimated or replicated' and that he 'never took the obvious path, both in music and in life', while Rod said how saddened he was by the death of his old bandmate, 'a gentleman and a truly unique character'.[21]

Since the name was collectively agreed on by the original five members in 1970, Lindisfarne have remained active with one line-up or another for over thirty of the intervening years. It is an achievement of which all members of the group, past and present, can remain proud, to say nothing of a formidable and long-lasting back catalogue of music. 'We became minstrels for the North East, reflecting what was happening there, and people felt a connection with us because we wrote about them, rather than writing about ephemeral things,' Ray said not long ago, 'We never set out to be pop stars or celebrities. We just wanted to be respected as musicians; we never planned to write 'singles'; we wrote albums. That was our philosophy.'[22] When asked at around the same time if he felt it was important for the group not to take themselves too seriously, he said that the important thing to them was the freedom to play their music and entertain people.[23] Alan's status as a Tyneside John Lennon had long been secure, as had his influence on songwriters from Elvis Costello—who has often praised 'Winter Song' as one of the best songs ever written, and performed it solo from time to time—and Noel Gallagher. It has also been suggested that the sound of Lindisfarne can be heard in Mumford & Sons, perhaps Britain's nearest equivalent in the twenty-first century.[24]

How long will the group, now in their fifth decade, stay on the road? Basically as long as they enjoy it and can physically do so, said Rod:

There is a lot of work behind the scenes—apart from the obvious rehearsing and the logistics of going on the road, there's a lot of promo and social media stuff that artists are expected to be proactive in nowadays. Fortunately, we have skills within the band which can meet those expectations and as long as there's time to do it properly, it can be positive and enjoyable and I like to think we do it well. We also have the advantage of being a bunch of mates who respect each other and are all pursuing the same end, much as the original band was; we have a great repertoire of songs—some very well-known, others less so but people recognise them when they hear them—so there's no pressure to come up with new songs or release an album every year (though I don't rule out the possibility of new material in the future); and we don't need to go out on tour more than we feel comfortable with. The old 40-date tours are a thing of the past. We tend now to go out on weekend jaunts and pick gigs which we fancy, because they're interesting and suit the vibe of the band.[25]

Endnotes

Abbreviations:

AH: Alan Hull
BM: Billy Mitchell
KC: Kenny Craddock
LOW: Lindisfarne official website
MM: *Melody Maker*
NME: *New Musical Express*
Q&A: Lindisfarne Question & Answer Archives, lindisfarnechat.
    myfreeforum.org/index.php
RC: Rod Clements
RC em: Rod Clements e-mails to author, July–August 2016
RJ: Ray Jackson
RL: Ray Laidlaw
RL em: Ray Laidlaw e-mails to author, August–November 2016
SC: Si Cowe
SD: Steve Daggett

Chapter 1

1. Harper, C., *Dazzling Stranger*, p. 18
2. *Record Mirror*, 22 January 1972, RJ to Keith Altham
3. *Sounds*, 27 May 1972, AH to Jerry Gilbert
4. Hill, D. I., *Fog on the Tyne*, p. 21
5. *NME*, 4 December 1971, AH to Roy Carr
6. LOW, 1 November 1989, 'Amigos' Track by track, AH
7. *NME*, 22.7.78 AH to Bob Edmands
8. *Sounds*, 27.5.1972, AH to Jerry Gilbert
9. *Ibid.*

10. *Disc & Music Echo*, 18.11.1972, AH to Andrew Tyler
11. *Rock 'n' Reel*, April 1996, 'Cat O'Tyne Tales', Simon Jones
12. Get Ready To Rock!, 25 May 2013, RJ to David Wilson
13. *Sounds*, 27 May 1972, AH to Jerry Gilbert
14. RC em
15. RL em
16. LOW, March 2004, RJ to Chris Kelly
17. *Rock 'n' Reel*, April 1996, 'Cat O'Tyne Tales', Simon Jones
18. LOW, March 2004, RJ to Chris Kelly

Chapter 2

1. LOW, Q&A, RL
2. Harper, C., *Dazzling Stranger*, p. 246
3. LOW, 'Marquee Memories', Chris Groom
4. *Ibid.*
5. LOW, Q&A, RL
6. Hill, D. I., *Fog on the Tyne*, p. 33
7. *Sounds*, 27 May 1972, AH to Jerry Gilbert
8. Ne4me, 23 November 2010, RL to Michael Hamilton
9. *The Times*, 18 November 1971, AH to Michael Wale
10. Thompson, D., *Blockbuster!* p. 219
11. *Go-Set*, 11 August 1973, AH to Steve Clarke
12. LOW, SC to Reinhard Groll, June 2001
13. RC em
14. Ne4me, 18 December 2010, SC to Michael Hamilton
15. LOW, 'Marquee Memories', Chris Groom
16. Dickson, B., *A Shirt Box Full of Songs*, p. 79
17. Young, R., *Electric Eden*, p. 552
18. *Sounds*, 24 November 1970
19. *MM*, Michael Watts, 24 November 1970
20. Hill, D. I., p. 38
21. *Ibid.*, p. 39
22. *The Times*, 26 January 1972, Michael Wale, Lyceum Concert review
23. LOW, Q&A, RL
24. Hill, D. I., p. 42
25. LOW, 'Marquee Memories', Chris Groom
26. RC em
27. Hill, D. I., p. 44
28. *Ibid.*
29. Stewart, R., *Rod: The Autobiography*, p. 120

Chapter 3

1. *Disc & Music Echo*, 2 February 1972, AH to Caroline Boucher; *Northern Correspondent*, 13 October 2015
2. Hill, D. I., *Fog on the Tyne*, p. 51
3. *MM*, 18 December 1971, SC to Jerry Gilbert
4. *Newcastle Evening Journal*, 2 May 2014, RC to Sam Wonfor
5. *NME*, 30 October 1971, RL to Pamela Holman
6. *Disc & Music Echo*, 22 January 1972, RJ to Michael Clayton
7. LOW, Q&A, RL
8. *Record Mirror*, 11 March 1972, AH to Keith Altham
9. Ne4me, 18 December 2010, RL to Michael Hamilton
10. *Ibid.*
11. *Sounds*, 27 May 1972, AH to Jerry Gilbert
12. *Record Mirror*, 3 June 1972, RC
13. *Ibid.*
14. *NME*, 13 May 1972, AH to Tony Stewart
15. Hill, D. I., p. 60
16. *The Press*, 30 September 2015, RL
17. Hill, D. I., p. 62
18. RL em
19. *Go-Set*, 11 August 1973, AH to Steve Clarke
20. *Record Mirror*, 3 June 1972, RC
21. LOW, Q&A, RL
22. *Daily Telegraph*, 20 November 1995, AH Obituary
23. *Disc & Music Echo*, 18 November 1972, SC to Andrew Tyler
24. LOW, Q&A, RL
25. *Ibid.*
26. *Go-Set*, 11 August 1973, AH to Steve Clarke
27. *Disc & Music Echo*, 1973, exact date unknown, AH to Rosalind Russell

Chapter 4

1. LOW, 13 October 1997, KC to Chris Groom
2. *Disc & Music Echo*, 1973, exact date unknown, RJ to Michael Clayton
3. LOW, Q&A, CH
4. Tobler, J., & Grundy, S., *The Record Producers*, pp. 213-4
5. *Disc & Music Echo*, 1973, exact date unknown, AH to Rosalind Russell

6. *Go-Set*, 11 August 1973, AH to Steve Clarke
7. Tobler, J., & Grundy, S., p. 213
8. Hill, D. I., *Fog on the Tyne*,p. 70
9. *Disc & Music Echo*, 1973, exact date unknown, RJ to Michael Clayton
10. RL em
11. LOW, 13 October 1997, KC to Chris Groom
12. *Sounds*, 10 November 1973, Jerry Gilbert
13. LOW, 13 October 1997, KC to Chris Groom
14. *Ibid.*
15. LOW, Q&A, RL
16. RC em
17. RL em
18. *Sounds*, 1973, exact date unknown
19. *Ibid.*
20. Hill, D. I., p. 75
21. LOW, SC to Reinhard Groll, June 2001
22. Hill, D. I., p. 78
23. *Ibid.*, p. 71
24. Review by Steve Clark, publication unknown
25. Hill, D. I., p. 71
26. *NME*, AH, 1 February 1975
27. LOW, Q&A, RJ
28. Hill, D. I., p. 71
29. *Ibid.*, p. 84
30. *Sounds*, 1 March 1975; Peel, J., *Olivetti Chronicles*, pp. 263-4
31. LOW, Q&A, BM
32. *Ibid.*
33. *Ibid.*
34. LOW, Q&A, RL

Chapter 5

1. Ne4me, 18.12.2010, RJ to Michael Hamilton
2. *NME*, AH to Bob Edmands, 22 July 1978
3 RL em
4. LOW, Q&A, RL
5. SC interview with Reinhard Groll, 2001
6. LOW, Q&A, RL
7. *NME*, AH to Bob Edmands, 22 July 1978
8. Hill, D. I., *Fog on the Tyne*, p. 97
9. LOW, Q&A, RJ

10. RJ Chris Kelly interview autumn 2005
11. LOW, Q&A, RL
12. LOW, 19 November 2001, 'A Memorial for Alan Hull'
13. Ne4me, 23 November 2010
14. Hill, D. I., p. 112
15. *The Times*, 16 March 1985
16. RC em
17. LOW, SD interview, Chris Groom and Reinhard Groll, February 2002
18. RC em
19. *The Times*, 20 November 1995, AH Obituary
20. Harper, C., *Dazzling Stranger*, p. 279
21. *Ibid.*, p. 281
22. RC em
23. SD interview 2002
24. *Amigos*, track by track, 1 November 1989

Chapter 6

1. LOW, Q&A, RJ
2. *Ibid.*
3. *Ibid.*
4. Ne4me, 18.12.2010, Jacka to Michael Hamilton
5. Hill, D. I., *Fog on the Tyne*, p. 124
6. RL em
7. LOW, RJ to Chris Kelly, autumn 2005
8. *Daily Telegraph*, 20.11.1995, AH Obituary
9. LOW, SD to Chris Groom, Reinhard Groll, February 2002
10. Hill, D. I., p. 126
11. *Where?* November 1991, RC to Tim Joseph
12 *Rock 'n' Reel*, April 1996, 'Cat O'Tyne Tales', Simon Jones
13 LOW, 13 October 1997, KC to Chris Groom
14. Hill, D. I., p. 130
15. LOW, 13 October 1997, KC to Chris Groom
16. *The Times*, 6 December 1994
17. *The Independent*, 7 July 2010
18. *The Times*, 2 August 1995
19. *Rock 'n' Reel*, April 1996, 'Cat O'Tyne Tales', Simon Jones
20. www.parliament.uk Early Day Motion 67, 20 November 1995
21. *Newcastle Evening Journal*, 25 November 1995
22. Ne4me, 18 December 2010, RL to Michael Hamilton
23. LOW, Q&A, RL

Chapter 7

1. Ne4me, 23 November 2010, RL
2. LOW, Q&A, RL
3. *Newcastle Evening Journal*, 2 May 2014, RC to Sam Wonfor, 2 May 2014
4. Hill, D. I., *Fog on the Tyne*, p. 148
5. LOW, Q&A, BM
6. *Arizona Daily Star*, 11-18 June 1999
7. *Ibid.*
8. LOW, SC to Reinhard Groll, June 2001
9. *Daily Mail*, 18 November 2011
10. *Newcastle Evening Journal*, 20 November 1995
11. LOW, 17 May 2004, Bob Templeman
12. RC em
13. LOW, Q&A, RL
14. *Newcastle Evening Journal*, 2 May 2014, RC to Sam Wonfor
15. *Ibid.*
16. LOW, 23.11.2001, 21 November 2011, 'A Memorial for Alan Hull'
17. *Newcastle Chronicle*, 19 December 2014, RJ to Sam Wonfor
18. *The Press*, 30.9.2015
19. Get Ready To Rock!, 25 May 2013, RJ to David Wilson
20. *Northern Echo*, 14 September 2013, RJ to Matt Westcott; Stewart, R., *Rod: The Autobiography*, p. 83
21. Alan's Album Archives, 2 October 2015, SC Obituary
22. *The Press*, 30 September 2015, RL
23. Get Ready To Rock!, 25 May 2013, RJ to David Wilson
24. Hepworth, D., *1971*, p. 345
25. RC em

Discography

Included below are month (if known) and year of release, and UK label except in the cases of material released overseas only. Bootlegs are excluded. For reasons of space, only the most important reissues and live sets are included, while guest appearances on records by other artists are restricted to those by the five original members only. Track listings for compilations and live sets containing only previously released material are not given. All singles and albums are on vinyl up to 1990, and on CD thereafter. Albums released simultaneously on LP and CD in the 1980s have identical track listings. Further information and details are available on the 45cat and Discogs websites cited in the Bibliography.

Lindisfarne

Albums

Nicely out of Tune: 'Lady Eleanor/Road to Kingdom Come/Winter Song/ Turn a Deaf Ear/Clear White Light/We Can Swing Together/Alan in the River With Flowers/Down/The Things I Should Have Said/Jackhammer Blues/Scarecrow Song' (Charisma, November 1970)
CD reissue, Charisma 2004, bonus tracks 'Knacker's Yard Blues/Nothing But The Marvellous Is Beautiful'

Fog on the Tyne: 'Meet Me on the Corner/Alright on the Night/Uncle Sam/ Together Forever/January Song/Peter Brophy Don't Care/City Song/ Passing Ghosts/Train in G Major/Fog on the Tyne' (Charisma, October 1971)
CD reissue, Charisma 2004, bonus tracks 'Scotch Mist/No Time to Lose'

Dingly Dell: 'All Fall Down/Plankton's Lament/Bring Down the Government/Poor Old Ireland/Don't Ask Me/Oh, No, Not Again/

Dingle Regatta/Wake Up Little Sister/Go Back/Court in the Act/
Mandolin King/Dingly Dell' (Charisma, September 1972)
CD reissue, Charisma 2004, bonus track 'We Can Swing Together (live)'
(seven-minute edit from B-side of 'All Fall Down' single)

Roll on, Ruby: 'Taking Care of Business/North Country Boy/Steppenwolf/
Nobody Loves You Anymore/When the War is Over/Moonshine/Lazy/
Roll On River/Toe the Line/Goodbye' (Charisma, November 1973)
CD reissue, Charisma 2004, bonus tracks 'Dealer's Choice/Tonight/You
Put the Laff on Me/In Your Hand'

Happy Daze: 'Tonight/In My Head/River/You Put the Laff on Me/No
Need to Tell Me/Juiced Up to Lose/Dealer's Choice/Nellie/The Man
Down There/Gin and Tonix All Round/Tomorrow' (Warner Bros,
September 1974)
CD reissue, Market Square 2008, bonus tracks 'Dingly Dell/Where Is My
Sixpence?/Do Not Be Afraid/Smile/Picture a Little Girl/Doctor of Love/
Alright on the Night'

Back and Fourth: 'Juke Box Gypsy/Warm Feeling/Woman/Only Alone/
Run for Home/King's Cross Blues/Get Wise/You and Me/Marshall
Riley's Army/Angels at Eleven/Make Me Want to Stay' (Mercury, June
1978)
CD reissue, Esoteric/Cherry Red 2012, bonus tracks 'Stick Together/When
it Gets the Hardest'

The News: 'Call of the Wild/People Say/1983/Log on Your Fire/Evening/
Easy and Free/Miracles/When Friday Comes Along/Dedicated Hound/
This Has Got to End/Good to be Here?' (Mercury, September 1979)

Sleepless Nights: 'Nights/Start Again/Cruising to Disaster/Same Way
Down/Winning the Game/About You/Sunderland Boys/Love is a Pain/
Do What I Want/Never Miss the Water/I Must Stop Going to Parties/
Stormy Weather' (LMP, October 1982)

Dance Your Life Away: 'Shine On/Love on the Run/Heroes/All in the Same
Boat/Dance Your Life Away/Beautiful Day/Broken Doll/100 Miles to
Liverpool/Take Your Time/Song for a Stranger' (River City, October
1986)

C'Mon Everybody: 'Let's Dance||New Orleans||Splish Splash/Party
Doll/You Never Can Tell/Little Bitty Pretty One/Running Bear||Mr

Bassman‖Sea Cruise/Let's Go‖Wooly Bully/C'Mon Everybody‖Do You Wanna Dance?‖Twist and Shout‖Do You Love Me/Runaround Sue/Shake Rattle and Roll‖See You Later Alligator/It'll Be Me‖You Keep A Knockin'/Love You More Than I Can Say/Oh Donna/ Keep Your Hands Off My Baby/Rhythm of the Rain/Speedy Gonzales‖Little Darlin'‖Dreamin'‖La Bamba/Meet Me on the Corner/Lady Eleanor/Fog on the Tyne/Run For Home/Warm Feeling/ Clear White Light' (Stylus, November 1987) (‖ denotes songs segued together)

Amigos: 'One World/Everything Changes/Working for the Man/Roll On That Day/You're the One/Wish You Were Here/Do It Like This/Anyway the Wind Blows/Strange Affair/When the Night Comes Down/Don't Say Goodnight/Another World (Black Crow, 1989)

Elvis Lives on the Moon: 'Day of the Jackal/Soho Square/Old Peculiar Feeling/Mother Russia/Demons/Don't Leave Me Tonight/Elvis Lives on the Moon/Keeping the Rage/Heaven Waits/Spoken Like a Man/Think' (Castle/Essential, 1993)

Here Comes the Neighbourhood: 'Born at the Right Time/Ghost in Blue Suede Shoes/Jubilee Corner/Can't do Right for Doing Wrong/Working My Way Back Home/Wejibileng/Unmarked Car/Devil of the North/ Uncle Henry/One Day/Driftin' Through' (Park, 1998)

Promenade: 'This Guitar Never Lies/When Jones Gets Back to Town/This Too Will Pass/Coming Good/Candlelight/Freedom Square/Under the Promenade/Rock 'n' Roll Phone/Unfinished Business/Happy Birthday Dad/Walking Back to Blueberry Hill/Significant Other/Remember Tomorrow' (Park, 2002)

Compilations and Radio Sessions
The Peel Sessions (Strange Fruit, 1988)

City Songs: BBC Sessions 1971-72 (BBC, 1988)

Buried Treasures, Vol. 1: 'Red Square Dance (Defectors)/Finest Hour/ Together Forever/Happy or Sad/Way Behind You (Brethren)/Old Peculiar Feeling/True Love/City Song/Rock 'n' Roll Town/Swiss Maid (Pacamax)/Sporting Life Blues (Downtown Faction)/Karen Marie/From My Window/Run Jimmy Run/Malvinas Melody/Let's Dance' (Virgin, 1992)—all Lindisfarne unless stated otherwise

Buried Treasures, Vol. 2: 'Save Our Ales/Ale Crack/Golden Apples/Apple
   Crack/Try Giving Everything (Geordie Aid)/Nothing's Gonna Break Us
   Now/January Song/Living on a Baseline/On My Own I Built a Bridge/
   Bridge Crack/Roll On That Day/Loving Around the Clock (Downtown
   Faction)/Reunion/Reunion Crack/Friday Girl/Tomorrow, If I'm Hungry
   (Alan Hull)/Hungry Crack/Fog on the Tyne (Pudding Mix)/Peter
   Gunn Theme‖Winning The Game (live)/Run For Home (live)' (Virgin,
   1992)—all Lindisfarne unless stated otherwise

Dealers Choice: BBC sessions 1973–4 (New Millennium Communications
   Ltd, 1998)

BT3: 'Positive Earth (Brethren)/100 Miles to Liverpool/Money/2 Way Street/
   Newport Mount Rag (Rod Clements and Mark Knopfler)/Poor Old
   Ireland/Corporation Rock/The One and Only (Lindisfarne featuring Little
   Mo)/Drinking Song/Heaven Waits/Log On Your Fire/Dragon of Dreamland
   (Alan Hull)/Checkin' On My Baby (Downtown Faction)/January Song
   (Lindisfarne featuring Fran Healy)/We've Got All Night/Digging Holes
   (Lindisfarne featuring Chris While and Julie Matthews)/Meet Me on the
   Corner (Siren, 2000)'—all Lindisfarne unless stated otherwise

At the BBC: The Charisma Years 1971–1973 (EMI, 2009)

The following compilations all contain previously released material:

Finest Hour (Charisma, 1975)
Lady Eleanor (Pickwick, 1976)
Repeat Performance: The Singles Album (Charisma, 1981)
Anthology: Road to Kingdom Come (Essential, 2000)
The Very Best of Lindisfarne (EMI Gold, 2003)
The Best of Lindisfarne (Virgin/Charisma, 2005)
The Collection: Meet Me on the Corner (Sanctuary Midline, 2006)
The Other Side of Lindisfarne (Mooncrest, 2006)—comprising tracks
   from side 3 and 4, or the second CD, of *C'Mon Everybody*

Live

Lindisfarne Live: 'No Time to Lose/Meet Me on the Corner/Alright on
   the Night/Train in G Major/Fog on the Tyne/We Can Swing Together/
   Jackhammer Blues' (Charisma, 1973)

Lindisfarne Live, The Definitive Edition: 'Intro/Together Forever/No Time
   to Lose/January Song/Meet Me on the Corner/Alright on the Night/

Train in G Major/Scotch Mist/Lady Eleanor/Knacker's Yard Blues/
Fog on the Tyne/We Can Swing Together/Jackhammer Blues/Clear
White Light' (Charisma/EMI, 2005)—reissue of previous album with
additional tracks

Magic in the Air: 'Lady Eleanor/Road to Kingdom Come/Turn a Deaf Ear/
January Song/Court in the Act/No Time to Lose/Winter Song/Uncle
Sam/Wake Up Little Sister/All Fall Down/Meet Me on the Corner/Bye
Bye Birdie/Train in G Major/Scarecrow Song/Dingly Dell/Scotch Mist/
We Can Swing Together/Fog on the Tyne/Clear White Light' (Mercury,
November 1978)

Lindisfarntastic! Live: 'I Must Stop Going to Parties/Marshal Riley's
Army/Down/We Can Swing Together/Fog on the Tyne/Engine Trouble/
Meet Me on the Corner/Clear White Light' (LMP, 1983)

Lindisfarntastic! Two: 'Moving House/Taxman/Lady Eleanor/Nights/Mr
Inbetween/Brand New Day/Mystery Play/Lover Not a Fighter/Day of
the Jackal/Stormy Weather' (LMP, 1984)

Another Fine Mess: 'Clear White Light (Part 2)/Squire/Lady Eleanor/Meet
Me on the Corner/Evening/City Song/One World/All Fall Down/Winter
Song/This Heart of Mine/We Can Make It/Road to Kingdom Come/
Money/Run for Home/Fog on the Tyne' (Grapevine, 1995)

Live at the Cambridge Folk Festival: 'Start Again/I Remember the Nights/
Lady Eleanor/Warm Feeling/Stormy Weather/Meet Me on the Corner/
I'm a Lover Not a Fighter/Winning the Game/Clear White Light (Part
2)/Run for Home/Fog on the Tyne/No Time to Lose' (Strange Fruit,
1996)

Tre Cropredy Festival: 'Road To Kingdom Come/All Fall Down/Elvis
Lives on the Moon/City Song/Evening/Day of the Jackal/We Can Make
It/Train in G Major/Walk in the Sea/Drinking Song/Meet Me on the
Corner/Run for Home/Clear White Light (Part 2)' (Mooncrest, 1997)

Untapped and Acoustic: 'No Time to Lose/Why Can't I Be Satisfied/
Sundown Station/Uncle Sam/Run for Home/Walk a Crooked
Mile/Scotch Mist/Bring Down the Government/Call of the Wild/
Passing Ghosts/United States of Mind/Lady Eleanor/Winter Song/
Dingle Regatta/We Can Swing Together' (River City, 1997)—reissued
1999 with additional tracks/100 Miles to Liverpool/Court in the Act/

Coming Home to You/Refugees/Knackers Yard Blues/Ardnamurchan'
(Park, 1999)

Boxed Set

The Charisma Years 1970–1973: Disc 1: Nicely out of Tune, tracks as CD
reissue above, plus bonus tracks 'From My Window (outtake)/ On My
Own I Built a Bridge (outtake)/Lady Eleanor (US mix)/ We Can Swing
Together (US mix)/Scarecrow Song (US mix)/Meet Me on the Corner
(demo version)'; *Disc 2: Fog on the Tyne*, tracks as CD reissue above,
plus bonus track 'January Song (extended version)'; *Dingly Dell*, tracks
as 1972 release; *Disc 3: Lindisfarne Live, The Definitive Edition*, tracks
as CD reissue above; *Disc 4: Roll On, Ruby*, tracks as CD reissue above
(Charisma/EMI, 2013)

Singles and EPs

'Clear White Light (Part 2)/Knacker's Yard Blues' (Charisma, Nov 1970)
'Lady Eleanor/Nothing but the Marvellous is Beautiful' (Charisma, May
    1971, reactivated May 1972)
'Meet Me on the Corner/Scotch Mist/No Time to Lose' (Charisma, Feb
    1972)
'All Fall Down/We Can Swing Together (live)' (Charisma, Sept 1972)
'Court in the Act/Don't Ask Me' (Charisma, Nov 1972)
'Taking Care of Business/North Country Boy' (Charisma, Mar 1974)
'Fog on the Tyne/Mandolin King' (Charisma, Jul 1974)
'Tonight/No Need to Tell Me' (Warner Bros, Nov 1974)
'Lady Eleanor/Fog on the Tyne' (Charisma, Nov 1975)
'Run for Home/Stick Together' (Mercury, Apr 1978)
'Juke Box Gypsy/When it Gets the Hardest' (Mercury, Sept 1978)
'Brand New Day/Winter Song (live)' (Mercury, Nov 1978)
'Warm Feeling/Clear White Light (live)' (Mercury, Feb 1979)
'Easy and Free/When Friday Comes Along' (Mercury, Aug 1979)
'Call of the Wild/Dedicated Hound' (Mercury, Oct 1979)
'Friday Girl/1983' (Subterranean, June 1980)
'I Must Stop Going to Parties/See How They Run' (Hangover, Nov 1981)
'Sunderland Boys/Cruising to Disaster' (LMP, Oct 1982)
'Nights/Dog Ruff' (LMP, Jan 1983)
'I Do What I Want/Same Way Down' (LMP, 1983)
'I Remember the Nights/Day of the Jackal' (LMP, 1985)
Christmas EP: 'Warm Feeling (live)/Red Square Dance/Run for Home
    (live)/Nights (acapella)' (LMP, Dec 1985)
'Shine On/Heroes/Dance Your Life Away' (River City, Oct 1986)
'Love on the Run/100 Miles to Liverpool' (River City, Feb 1987)

'Party Doll/C'Mon Everybody (medley)/Do You Wanna Dance/Twist and Shout/Do You Love Me' (Honey Bee, Nov 1987)

'Save Our Ales/Save Our Ales (Sub Mix)' (River City, 1988)

'Lady Eleanor '88/Meet Me on the Corner' (Virgin, Nov 1988)

'Do It Like This/Roll on That Day/I Must Stop Going to Parties (1990 Cake Mix)' (Black Crow, Oct 1989)

'Day of the Jackal/Demons' (Essential, 1993)

Blues From The Bothy EP: 'Coming Home to You/Refugees/Knackers Yard Blues/Ardnamurchan' (River City, Aug 1997)

Gazza and Lindisfarne Singles

'Fog on the Tyne (Revisited)/Fog on the Tyne (Revisited) (Instrumental)' (Best, October 1990)

'Geordie Boys (Gazza Rap)/Fog on the Tyne (Revisited) (Gazza Golden Goals Mix)' (Best, December 1990)—Lindisfarne B-side only

Alan Hull

Albums

Pipedream: 'Breakfast/Justanothersadsong/Money Game/STD 0632/ United States of Mind/Country Gentleman's Wife/Numbers (Travelling Band)/For the Bairns/Drug Song/Song for a Windmill/Blue Murder/I Hate to See You Cry' (Charisma, 1973)

CD reissue Charisma 2005, bonus tracks 'Drinking Song/One Off Pat/ Down on the Underground/Gin and Tonix All Round/Dan the Plan'

Squire: 'Dan the Plan/Picture a Little Girl/Ain't Nothin' Shakin' (But the Leaves on the Trees)/One More Bottle of Wine/Golden Oldies/I'm Sorry/ Squire/Waiting/Bad Side of Town/Mr Inbetween/The End' (Warner Bros, 1975)

CD reissue Esoteric/Cherry Red 2013, bonus tracks 'Crazy Woman/ Carousel'

Phantoms: I Wish You Well/Anywhere is Everywhere/Make Me Want to Stay/Dancing on the Judgement Day/A Walk in the Sea/Corporation Rock/Madmen and Loonies/Somewhere Out There/Love is the Alibi/ Love is the Answer' (Rocket, 1979)

CD reissue Market Square 2007, bonus tracks 'Isn't It Strange/Spittin' in the Wind/Lay Back and Dream/Something Got the Better of You/ Somewhere Out There (demo)/Raw Bacon (demo)/A Walk in the Sea (demo)/Evening (demo)/Dancing on the Judgement Day (demo)'

On the Other Side: 'On the Other Side/Evergreen/Inside a Broken Heart/
   Malvinas Melody/American Man/A Mystery Play/Day of the Jackal/
   Love in a Cage/Fly Away' (Black Crow, 1983)

Statues and Liberties: 'Statues & Liberties/Walk a Crooked Mile/
   Cardboard Christmas Boxes/Treat Me Kindly/100 Miles To Liverpool/
   Money/This Heart of Mine/Long Way From Home/When the Sun Goes
   Down/Hoi Poloi/Save Yourself/Drug Song' (Castle Communications,
   1996)

When the War is Over: The BBC Recordings 1973 &1975: 'Drug Song/
   Numbers (Travelling Band)/United States of Mind/When the War is
   Over/Down on the Underground/Gin and Tonics All Around/One More
   Bottle of Wine/Dan the Plan/Dealer's Choice/Winter Song/One More
   Bottle of Wine/Peter Brophy Don't Care/The Squire/City Song/Dan the
   Plan/Money Game/Gin and Tonics All Around/One More Bottle Of
   Wine/Golden Oldies/Dealer's Choice/Alright on the Night' (BBC, 1998)

We Can Swing Together: The Anthology 1965–1995: 'I Won't Be Around
   You Any More[1]/Big City[1]/So Much to Look Forward To[1]/Today, Tonight
   & Tomorrow[1]/This We Shall Explore[2]/Schizoid Revolution[2]/Where is my
   Sixpence?[3]/We Can Swing Together[3]/Obidiah's Grave[3]/Lady Eleanor[4]/
   Winter Song[4]/Fog on the Tyne[4]/Poor Old Ireland[4]/All Fall Down (live) [4]/
   Court in the Act (live)[4]/Money Game[3]/Justanothersadsong[3]/Taking Care
   of Business[4]/Squire[3]/Dan the Plan[3]/I Wish You Well[5]/Run for Home[4]/
   Jukebox Gypsy[4]/Marshall Riley's Army[4]/Call of the Wild[4]/Shine On[4]/
   Heroes[4]/One Hundred Miles to Liverpool[4]/Elvis Lives on the Moon[4]/
   Spoken like a Man[4]/Soho Square[4]/Day of the Jackal[4]/We Can Make It[4]/
   United States of Mind[3]/Breakfast (live)[3]/Oh No Not Again (live)[3]/Hoi
   Poloi[3]/Walk a Crooked Mile[3]/Statues & Liberties[3]/Clear White Light
   (live)[4]' (Castle, 2005)
   1. The Chosen Few
   2. Alan Hull with Skip Bifferty
   3. Alan Hull
   4. Lindisfarne
   5. Radiator

The Alan Hull Songbook: Some Other Time: 'Some Other Time/Never be
   the Same from Today/Click-Clock Tick-Tock/Little Things/Love Lasts
   Forever/Clear White Light/Wild Flowers/297 Words/Personal History
   Book/Opposites/I am and So Are You/She' (Belvue, 2016)—Hull's songs
   performed by Dave Hull-Denholm, Ian Thomson, Bradley Creswick

Live

Another Little Adventure: 'Drinking Song/Money Game/United States of Mind/Dan the Plan/Treat Me Kindly/Fly Away/Malvinas Melody/One More Bottle of Wine/Poor Old Ireland/Evening/January Song/All Fall Down/Marshall Riley's Army/Heroes' (Black Crow, 1988)

Back to Basic: 'United States of Mind/Poor Old Ireland/All Fall Down/Lady Eleanor/Winter Song/Walk in the Sea/Mother Russia/This Heart of Mine/Mr Inbetween/January Song/Breakfast/Day of the Jackal/Oh No Not Again/Run for Home/Fog on the Tyne' (Mooncrest, 1994)

Alright on the Night: 'Squire/City Song/Dan the Plan/Breakfast/Money Game/January Song/Cheeky Mouse/Gin and Tonix All Around/One More Bottle of Wine/Winter Song/Alright on the Night/We Can Swing Together/Fog on the Tyne/Lady Eleanor' (Market Square, 2010)

Singles

'We Can Swing Together/Obidiah's Grave' (Transatlantic/Big T, 1969)
'Numbers (Travelling Band)/Drinking Song/One Off Pat' (Charisma, June 1973)
'Justanothersadsong/Waiting' (Charisma, Sept 1973)
'Dan the Plan/One More Bottle of Wine' (Warner Bros, 1975)
'One More Bottle of Wine/Squire' (Warner Bros, 1975)
'Crazy Woman/Golden Oldies' (Warner Bros, 1975)
'I Wish You Well/Love is the Answer' (Rocket, Apr 1979)
'A Walk in the Sea/Corporation Rock' (Rocket, Jul 1979)
'Malvinas Melody/Owed to a Taxman' (Black Crow, 1983)

Jack the Lad

Albums

It's...Jack the Lad: 'Boilermaker Blues/Back on the Road Again/Plain Dealing/Fast Lane Driver/Turning Into Winter/Why Can't I Be Satisfied/Song Without a Band/Rosalie/Promised Land/A Corny Pastiche (Medley)/The Black Cock of Wickham/Chief O'Neill's Favourite/The Golden Rivet/Staten Island/The Cook in the Kitchen/Lying on the Water' (Charisma, Mar 1974)
CD reissue Virgin/Charisma 1992, bonus tracks 'One More Dance/Make Me Happy'

The Old Straight Track: 'Oakey Strike Evictions/Jolly Beggar/The Third Millenium/Weary Whaling Grounds/Fingal the Giant/Kings Favourite/

The Marquis of Tullybardine/Peggy (Overseas with a Soldier)/Buy
Broom Buzzems/De Havilland's Mistake/The Old Straight Track/The
Wurm' (Charisma, Sept 1974)
CD reissue, Virgin/Charisma 1992, bonus tracks 'Home Sweet Home/Big
Ocean Liner'

Rough Diamonds: 'Rocking Chair/Smokers Coughin'/Captain Grant/My
Friend the Drink/A Letter from France/Gentleman Soldier/Gardener
of Eden/One for the Boy/The Beachcomber/The Ballad of Winston
O'Flaherty/Jackie Lusive' (Charisma, Jul 1975)
CD reissue Virgin/Charisma 1992, bonus tracks 'Draught Genius/Baby
Let Me Take You Home'

Jackpot: 'Eight Ton Crazy/Amsterdam/Steamboat Whistle Blues/Walter's
Drop/We'll Give You the Roll/Trinidad/You, You, You/Let It Be Me/The
Tender/Take Some Time' (United Artists, 1976)
CD reissue Market Square 2008, bonus tracks 'Trinidad (demo)/ See How
They Run (demo)/ Eight Ton Crazy (demo)/ Amsterdam (demo)/ Buy
Broom Buzzems||The Tender||The Marquis of Tullybardine (live)/ Will
You Miss Me (live)/Hungry for Love (live)'

Back on the Road Again (Live): 'Peggy (Overseas with a Soldier)/ Rocking
Chair/Buy Broom Buzzems/The Jolly Beggar/Steamboat Whistle Blues/
From a Jack to a King/Weary Whaling Grounds/The Ballad of Winston
O'Flaherty/Captain Grant/Why Can't I Be Satisfied/The Tender/
Gentleman Soldier/Walter's Drop' (Mah Mah 1993)—cassette only

Singles
'One More Dance/Draught Genius (Polka)' (Charisma, May 1973)
'Why Can't I Be Satisfied/Make Me Happy' (Charisma, Nov 1973)
'Home Sweet Home/Big Ocean Liner' (Charisma, Jan 1975)
'Gentleman Soldier/Oakey Strike Evictions' (Charisma, May 1975)
'Rocking Chair/My Friend the Drink' (Charisma, Oct 1975)
'Eight Ton Crazy/Walter's Drop' (United Artists, Sept 1976)
'Trinidad/Let It Be Me' (United Artists, Oct 1976)

Ray Jackson

Album
In the Night: 'Everything Will Turn Out Fine/Make it Last/In the Night/
Another Lonely Day/Stick Around Joe/Waiting for the Time/Little Town

Flirt/Tread on a Good Thing/You Send Me/Easy Love/Solo Again/In the Midnight Hour' (Mercury, Feb 1980)

Singles
'Take Some Time/Working On' (EMI, Aug 1976)
'In the Night/Waiting for the Time' (Mercury, Feb 1980)
'Little Town Flirt/Make It Last' (Mercury, Apr 1980)

Rod Clements

Albums
One Track Mind: 'Hard Travellin'/The Train that Carried My Girl from Town/Bourgeois Blues/Train in G Major/Ain't No More Cane/Down in the Flood/Road to Kingdom Come/Evil Hearted Woman/Meet Me on the Corner/Leather Launderette/No Turning Back/Sneaky Suspension/Piston Broke Again/Long Vehicle' (Limited edition available at gigs only, cassette 1994), CD reissue Siren 2001
CD reissue Batsville 2008, bonus tracks 'No Turning Back (home version)/A Dream within a Dream/Blues for a Dying Season'

Stamping Ground: 'Stamping Ground/Whisky Highway/Blue Interior/Hattie McDaniel at the Oscars 1939/Whole Lifestyle Thing/Charity Main/Roads of East Northumberland/Black Rain/We Have to Talk/Cowboy in the Rain/One More Night With You/Old Blue Goose' (Market Square, 2000)

Live Ghosts: 'Stamping Ground/Why Can't I Be Satisfied?/Blue Interior/Charity Main/Roads of East Northumberland/When Jones Gets Back to Town/Candlelight/Whole Lifestyle Thing/Remember Tomorrow/Can't do Right for Doing Wrong/Lost Highway/Meet Me on the Corner' (Batsville, Nov 2004)

Odd Man Out: 'All Grown Up & Nowhere to Go/Existentially Yours/Taking the Back Road Home/Dead Man's Karaoke/Odd Man Out/Touch-me-not/Ragtown/New Best Friend/September Sunrise/Morocco Bound' (Market Square, June 2006)

Rendezvous Café: 'Road to Kingdom Come/Train in G Major/Meet Me on the Corner/Don't Ask Me/Why Can't I Be Satisfied?/Plain Dealing/Sunderland Boys/Sundown Station/Any Way the Wind Blows/Roll on That Day/Old Peculiar Feeling/Refugees/Coming Home to You/Working

My Way Back Home/Ghost in Blue Suede Shoes/Jubilee Corner/Can't do Right for Doing Wrong/One Day/Unmarked Car/This Guitar Never Lies/When Jones Gets Back to Town/Candlelight/Unfinished Business/This Too Will Pass/Freedom Square/Remember Tomorrow' (Batsville, 2014)

Bert Jansch and Rod Clements

Album

Leather Launderette: 'Strolling Down the Highway/Sweet Rosie/Brafferton/Ain't No More Cane/Why Me?/ Sundown Station/Knight's Move/Brownsville/Bogie's Bonnie Belle/Leather Launderette/Been on the Road So Long' (Black Crow, 1988)

Radiator

Album

Isn't It Strange: 'Spittin' in the Wind/I Wish You Well/A Walk in the Sea/Madmen and Loonies/Corporation Rock/Isn't It Strange/Lay Back and Dream/Something Got the Better of You/Love is the Alibi/Love is the Answer' (Rocket, 1977)

Single

'Isn't It Strange/Dancing on the Judgement Day' (Rocket, May 1977)

Chosen Few

Singles

'I Won't Be Around You Any More/Big City' (Pye, Jul 1965)
'So Much to Look Forward To/Today, Tonight & Tomorrow' (Pye, Sept 1965)

The Defectors

'Red Square Dance/Dance of the Dissidents' (Red Square, 1980)

Alan Hull Guest Appearances

Robert Barton:	'Benwell Lad' (The Award Label, 1975)
Maxie & Mitch:	*Double Trouble* (Rubber, 1983)
Various artists:	*Take Off Your Head and Listen* (Rubber, 1971)
	Heroes (Rock'n'Dole, 1985)
	Sailing Home (River City, 1993)

Ray Jackson Guest appearances

Long John Baldry:	*It Ain't Easy* (Warner Bros, 1971)
Robert Barton:	'Benwell Lad' (The Award Label, 1974)
Breathe:	*Peace of Mind* (A&M, 1990)
Derek Brimstone:	*Shuffleboat River Farewell* (Rubber, 1976)
Chis de Burgh:	*Far Beyond These Castle Walls* (A&M, 1974)
Peter Hammill:	*Fool's Mate* (Charisma, 1971)
Mike Harding:	'My Brother Sylvest' (Rubber, 1975)
Rab Noakes:	*Red Pump Special* (Warner Bros, 1974)
Pete Scott:	*Jimmy the Moonlight* (Rubber, 1976)
Rod Stewart:	*Every Picture Tells a Story* (Mercury, 1971)
	Never a Dull Moment (Mercury, 1972)
	Smiler (Mercury, 1974)
Grethe Svenson:	*The Love of a Woman* (RCA, 1993) [Norway]
	Your Beauty (RCA, 1995) [Norway]
Various artists:	*Take Off Your Head and Listen* (Rubber, 1971)
	Woody Lives! A Tribute to Woody Guthrie (Black Crow, 1987)

Rod Clements Guest Appearances

Michael Chapman:	*The Man Who Hated Mornings* (Decca, 1977)
	Looking for Eleven (Criminal, 1980)
Wizz Jones:	*Happiness Was Free* (Intercord, 1976) [Germany]
Rick Kemp:	*Escape* (Fellside, 1997)
Ian McCallum:	*Left Handed* (Fat Mice, 1988) [Netherlands]
Ralph McTell:	*Streets* (Warner Bros, 1975)
	Right Side Up (Warner Bros, 1976)
Rab Noakes:	*Rab Noakes* (A&M, 1972)
	Under the Rain (Black Crow, 1984)
Pentangle:	*So Early in the Spring* (Making Waves, 1990)

Prelude: *Owlcreek Incident* (Dawn, 1975)
Nigel Stonier: *Golden Coins for the Holy Kid*
                          (Market Square, 1993)
Kathryn Tickell: *Borderlands* (Black Crow, 1986)
Various artists: *Woody Lives! A Tribute to Woody Guthrie*
                          (Black Crow, 1987)

Ray Laidlaw Guest Appearances

Michael Chapman: *Looking for Eleven* (Criminal, 1980)
                          Navigation (Planet, 1995)
Ralph McTell: *Songs from Alphabet Zoo* (Mays, 1983)
Rab Noakes: *Under the Rain* (Black Crow, 1984)
Various artists: *Sailing Home* (River City, 1993)

Bibliography

Books

Dickson, B., *A Shirt Box Full of Songs: The Autobiography* (Hachette Scotland, 2009)

Harper, C., *Dazzling Stranger: Bert Jansch and the British Folk And Blues Revival* (London: Bloomsbury, 2006)

Hepworth, D., *1971: Never A Dull Moment* (London: Bantam, 2016)

Hill, D.I., *Fog on the Tyne: The Official History of Lindisfarne* (Bordon: Northdown, 1998)

Laing, D., et al, *The Electric Muse: The Story of Folk into Rock* (London: Methuen, 1975)

Peel, J., *The Olivetti Chronicles: Three Decades of Life and Music* (London: Bantam, 2008)

Stewart, R., *Rod: The Autobiography* (London: Century, 2012)

Thompson, D., *Blockbuster! The True Story of The Sweet* (London: Cherry Red, 2010)

Tobler, J., & Grundy, S., *The Record Producers* (London: BBC, 1982)

Young, R., *Electric Eden: Unearthing Britain's Visionary Music* (London: Faber, 2011)

Newspapers and Journals

(all UK unless stated otherwise)
Arizona Daily Star (US)
Daily Telegraph
Daily Mail
Disc & Music Echo
Go-Set
Independent

Let It Rock
Melody Maker
Newcastle Evening Journal
New Musical Express
Northern Correspondent
Northern Echo
The Press, York
Record Collector
Record Mirror
Rock 'n' Reel
Sounds
The Times
Where? Magazine

Internet

All accessed April–August 2016

45cat, vinyl database: www.45cat.com
Alan's Album Archives: alansalbumarchives.blogspot.co.uk
Discogs, vinyl and CD database: www.discogs.com
Doug Morter official website dougmorter.com
Get Ready to Rock!: getreadytorock.me.uk
Lindisfarne official website: lindisfarne.co.uk
Ne4me—North-East England: www.ne4me.co.uk

Index